T0112642

The Tudor Tutor

Your Cheeky Guide to the Dynasty

BARB ALEXANDER

Illustrations by Lisa Graves

Skyhorse Publishing

Skyhorse Publishing books may be purchased in bulk at special discounts for sales promotion, corporate gifts, fund-raising, or educational purposes. Special editions can also be created to specifications. For details, contact the Special Sales Department, Skyhorse Publishing, 307 West 36th Street, 11th Floor, New York, NY 10018 or info@skyhorsepublishing.com.

Skyhorse® and Skyhorse Publishing® are registered trademarks of Skyhorse Publishing, Inc.®, a Delaware corporation.

Visit our website at www.skyhorsepublishing.com.

10 9 8 7 6 5 4 3 2

Library of Congress Cataloging-in-Publication Data is available on file.

Cover design by Anthony Morais

Print ISBN: 978-1-63450-402-7
Ebook ISBN: 978-1-63450-881-0

Printed in China

When I was a child and would spend the night at my grandmother's house, I'd ask her to tell me a "true story," a tale of her days growing up in South Philadelphia, before I went to sleep.

This book is dedicated to her, Gertie Presti, my most beloved part of my own history.

ILLUSTRATION KEY BY PAGE NUMBER

CONTENTS

Welcome!

You are about to enter the fifteenth, sixteenth, and seventeenth centuries.

Take care not to judge this time period by our twenty-first-century standards. This includes conventions on religious tolerance, crime and punishment, adultery, and parent-child relationships.

Please leave your desire for indoor plumbing, antibiotics, and good dental care behind.

Enjoy your journey!

In a Hurry?
Just the Basics

The Tudor dynasty began with the highly organized and fiscally responsible Henry VII, whose oldest son Arthur was meant to be the next king before he kicked the bucket at age fifteen. Henry's second son, the future Henry VIII, then became heir to the throne.

As you may recall, the charismatic and increasingly beefy Henry VIII was on a fierce mission to create a male heir. The only surviving one was to become Edward VI after his father's death.

Fifteen is an unlucky age for males in this family: When Edward was that age, he too died and his cousin Lady Jane Grey became queen for a short blip (nine days, to be exact). Edward's half-sister Mary wasn't taking that lying down. She executed Lady Jane and she soon became Mary I.

After engaging in behavior that would later inspire a tomato-based cocktail, Mary died childless, and her half-sister became Elizabeth I, easily identifiable by her cupcake-paper neck ruff and pasty complexion. Elizabeth too died childless; with all this family's bad luck in the health and reproductive departments, there were no other Tudors to step in. The crown went to James VI of Scotland (whose great-great grandfather was Henry VII). He became James I of England, and the Stuart dynasty began.

1

Henry VII: Who Died and Made Him King?

What is arguably the most interesting dynasty in English royal history almost never came to be. Before the Tudors of Wales became *the* Tudors, Richard III, head of the house of York, sat on the throne. But during one little battle, Henry Tudor and his guys swept in and finished him off with their weapons. When Richard III's bones were discovered under a Leicester parking lot in 2012, they showed evidence of fatal blows. A sword had entered his skull on one end and came out the other after slicing through his brain, and another segment of his skull had been whacked clear away. The king was dead, long live the new king, Henry VII!

But who did this Henry think he was? Primogeniture, the tradition of passing the crown on from father to oldest son, had been all the rage in England for about four hundred years. Richard III had no surviving heirs when he died and the rest of the children on the York side were either freshly dead (the little princes in the Tower) or female (definitely a problem). But how did Henry Tudor enter the picture?

First, let's talk about Henry himself. His mother, Margaret Beaufort (a powerhouse in an itty-bitty package) was pregnant with him at age thirteen, not unusual for that time period. His father was captured during the Wars of the Roses and died in prison, before his son was born. Even as a boy, this kid oozed self-confidence, so much so that Henry VI stated he was one to whom "both we and our adversaries must yield, and give over the domain." Though his mother remarried later, Henry spent a lot of time with his uncle Jasper, and it was Jasper who took him to France when he was a teenager. As someone with a claim to the throne, Henry was safer in France than in Wales.

The Wars of the Roses were a series of civil wars between two sides of the same family. (This is known today in some families as "the holidays.") The house of York was on one side; the house of Lancaster was on the other. This massive family feud carried on for about thirty years. Henry was the last surviving possibility for the Lancastrians, but the Yorkists were currently in charge in the form of Richard III.

Shortly after his dear brother, Edward IV, died (and Edward's son became Edward V), Richard took the throne for himself. He convinced Parliament that his two nephews were illegitimate because their father was betrothed to another woman before he married their mother. At that time, betrothal held as much weight as marriage, so Richard had no trouble declaring the boys bastards (so much for the one being Edward V; now he was just plain old Edward) and imprisoning them in the Tower of London.

Edward, age twelve, and Richard, age ten, have since been referred to as "the little princes in the Tower," who were seen in the grounds occasionally for a few months after their imprisonment . . . and then vanished altogether. In 1674, a chest containing the skeletons of two adolescents was found by workmen who were demolishing stairs leading to the White Tower. While the fate of the two princes has never been determined for certain, many believe these remains were the royal boys. If they were, in fact, murdered, and by whom, is one of English history's enduring mysteries to this day.

Usurper or not, Richard III had only been king for a scant two years when Henry Tudor felt the time was right and whipped up an army of fellow twenty-somethings, marching off to meet Richard and his own army in Leicestershire. Richard III, a seasoned military commander, charged down the hill with his men, who greatly outnumbered the Tudor troops. Henry's supporters assembled themselves into a human shield, which Richard et al hacked their way through laboriously with the intent of securing victory! But no dice: Richard was slain in nothing flat and died from the aforementioned wounds. And then, presto—there was Henry VII.

The new king, known to history as a frugal man, indulged in a rare splash-out for his coronation, a lush event intended to cement the image of the new dynasty and keep Richard—who?—from the minds of his subjects. He marketed himself as the "most Christian and most gracious prince, our most dread sovereign lord," well aware that an endorsement from

God Himself was good enough for those medieval subjects.

While careful and conservative, Henry VII was charming and elegant as well, a slim man with wavy brown shoulder-length hair and a penchant for speaking fluent French. This sophistication and culture would certainly be seen in his eventual heir, albeit alongside indulgence and gregariousness. The dignity of his reign would later be cemented as propaganda in the form of the imposing terra-cotta bust created by Pietro Torrigiano, made near the end of Henry's life.

Because family feuds are uncomfortable, and thirty years is a long time, Henry VII was clever enough to wrap up the Wars of the Roses by marrying Elizabeth of York, Richard III's niece and the only family member left on the York side. It was an opportunistic move at first: pair up with the girl from the other side of the conflict, relocate her mother to a nunnery, bring peace and happiness to all of England (except, of course, the mother in the nunnery, as well as Richard III's supporters).

Elizabeth's own father was military mastermind Edward IV, the first Yorkist king and father of the little princes, so she was certainly a fine catch from a fine background. Pairing up with Edward's daughter was a smart move on Henry Tudor's part, and the fulfillment of a promise he'd made to her mother, Elizabeth Woodville, who expected Henry to avenge the deaths of her sons, the little princes in the Tower. The Welshman was psyched to do so, and as word of the assumed murder of the princes spread, Richard III was becoming more unpopular by the day. This

created the perfect opportunity for Henry to make his move on the battlefield, and then in marriage.

The nice surprise for Henry VII was that his lovely blue-eyed blonde was kind, generous, liked to dance and hunt, and kept greyhounds. This was a refreshing combination in a medieval princess, and he couldn't pass it up. Unlike their successors, Henry VII and his Queen of Hearts didn't have fertility issues. Elizabeth gave birth to their first child, Prince Arthur, just eight months after their wedding. Six children followed, though only three survived into their teens.

The oldest girl, Margaret, was tearfully handed over to James IV of Scotland in marriage, in the hopes that England and Scotland could finally play nicely. Some years down the road, her husband and his army would head south to challenge Henry VIII and his control over that northern land. An arrow through the jaw later, at Flodden Field, James IV was no more, leaving his baby son and future father of Mary Queen of Scots as king of Scotland. Pay attention, because that point will be important later!

Another daughter, the lovely and spoiled Mary, was matched up with the elderly Louis XII of France. Just before she became *la reine*, she chatted to her brother about what her life would be like after the old king was dead. No dust on her!

She made it clear that she wanted Groom #2 to be Charles Brandon, her brother's gorgeous friend and the duke of Suffolk. Louis XII died only a few months after their wedding, reportedly of "exhaustions in the bed chamber," and Mary didn't waste much time in marrying Brandon. They eventually became grand-

parents to Lady Jane Grey, another significant fact that will come in handy later in the dynasty.

As for the heir, fifteen-year-old Arthur married a keeper, Catherine of Aragon. Her parents were Ferdinand and Isabella of Castile, so this pairing was golden for the Tudors. But just four months after their wedding, Arthur died suddenly. Less than a year after that, Elizabeth of York succumbed to complications after giving birth to a daughter, who also died soon after. Understandably, Henry VII was heartbroken and ducked out of public view completely for six weeks. He came down with an illness similar to tuberculosis and it nearly killed him. However, he bounced back and got on with the business of raising his new heir, Prince Henry.

In time, the king was encouraged to remarry for diplomatic reasons. Sensing that her daughter, Henry VII's widowed daughter-in-law Catherine of Aragon, might be in his line of vision, Isabella of Castille tried a distraction: "Hey look, over there, something shiny! It's Joan, Queen of Naples!" The king was interested enough to send his ambassadors to get the goods on Joan; he clearly wanted to know what he might be getting into. Aside from needing to know the height of her forehead and the possibility of hair on her upper lip, Henry told the ambassadors to answer the following questions: How was her complexion? Were her arms big or small, long or short? Was the palm of her hand thick or thin? Were her hands fat or lean, long or short? Were her fingers long or short, small or great, broad or narrow? Was her neck long or short, small or great?

Were her breasts big or small? You know, the usual concerns.

The answers were promising: Her complexion was clean, fair, and sanguine. Her arms were somewhat round and not very small, but "of good proportion to her personage and stature of height." Her hands were somewhat full, soft, fair, and clean-skinned, and her fingers were fair and small. Her neck was full and comely, not misshapen, not very short nor very long. However, it appeared shorter "because her breasts were full and somewhat big" as well as "highly trussed."

But it just didn't work out in the end, money and politics and all. There's no word on whether the king gave Joan the "it's not thee, it's me" speech.

Before long, his tuberculosis was back with a vengeance. His breathing was labored, his joints were racked with arthritis, and his final hours were spent beating himself up with guilt over the lives he'd destroyed. This well-organized micro-manager had been planning for his death ever since that first bout with TB, a decade earlier. When the disease finally won, Henry left England in a strong financial position, with a promising heir. What could possibly go wrong?

2

Henry VIII:
The Notorious HRH

Little Prince Henry was merely "the spare" in his royal family. Although he wasn't groomed to be king, he collected quite a few titles before the age of four: Lord Lieutenant of Ireland, Duke of York, Knight of the Garter, All-Around Lovely Chap.

Young Henry was an activity whirlwind: tennis, archery, jousting, fencing, wrestling—there was no shortage of physical outlets for the little prince. During the king's early years, the Venetian ambassador, Sebastian Guistinian marveled that "it is the prettiest thing in the world to see [Henry VIII] play [tennis]; his fair skin glowing through a shirt of the finest texture." One can only assume he was equally awe-inspiring while taking part in other sports, a departure from our image of an obese and sedentary madman.

His education was well-rounded; the kid was immersed in the Classics, math, reading, writing, and French. In later years, he'd stockpile books and devour their contents, donning his glasses when settling down to enjoying his reading time in his bed-chamber. Similarly, music (his forte) would follow him to adulthood, much to the benefit of Thomas Tallis, the versatile and prolific composer who enjoyed the patronage of not only Henry VIII but also the rest of the Tudor monarchs to follow.

Ultimately, the spare would not only step up to the plate when the heir dropped out, but he would also rock the monarchy (and the institution of marriage) in an unprecedented way. Five hundred years later, the man is still analyzed, lionized, criticized. On one hand, who goes to such measures simply for a son? What's wrong with girls? Maybe one of them would even amount to something great, who knows? And the whole smashing-up-the-monasteries thing, religious persecution, and battling it out with the Vatican—for what? For England? Maybe. His ego? Perhaps for a little of both: his bloodline.

Henry VIII—tyrant, serial husband, big-boned gastronome—was once a beloved little newborn in the royal Tudor household. As the second son, he was never meant to be king, and yet there he was after the untimely death of his older brother. (The Spanish ambassador reported that, upon Henry's accession, the people were as joyful as if they'd just made a prison break.)

Aside from being the cause of much celebration, this charming boy also needed to become the powerful ruler. Surrounded by friends, women, toadying courtiers, and low-lying enemies, he needed to navigate the waters and somehow pass on his genetic code to the more respected sex—by having boys, and lots of them.

While his father had the kingdom's paperwork well under control, other things vied for the new Henry's

attention: the aforementioned activities, theology, and carnal pleasures. He loved showing off the grandeur of his court and the fact that he was young, energetic, and hooked on opulence. His subjects adored rather than feared him. Guistinian, again, offered that Henry was "magnificent, liberal, and an enemy of the French." (Probably impressive for the English, but *pas grand-chose* for the French.) And Erasmus described him as "a man of gentle friendliness . . . more like a companion than a king."

Yet things got messy. The man is a legend after all these centuries partly because of the dichotomy that existed within him. Was he a monster? An egotistical maniac? A product of his time period and environment? His reputation precedes him; Henry VIII is probably the most notorious Tudor of all. And in a dynasty teeming with power struggles and other drama, that's no small feat.

SIZE MATTERS

Henry's weight is often a source of debate. There is the misconception that he had always been a tub of fun, chewing on a turkey leg and washing it down with gallons of mead. The truth is, young Henry was a vision of hotness, a trim and handsome prince who was to jousting what David Beckham became to soccer.

His armor, on display at the Tower of London, shows his weight gain from time period to time period. When he was twenty-three, his waist measured 34.7 inches; by age twenty-eight, it was up to 36

inches. During this time, he was married to Catherine of Aragon. He didn't marry Anne Boleyn until his early forties, and while at that point he wasn't necessarily still at underwear-model standards, he was not yet "fat."

In January 1536, the king was knocked from his horse during a jousting match. To add insult to injury, his armored horse landed right on top of him. That had to hurt. And it knocked him out for two hours to boot. Some historians believe this to be the point when Henry's personality started its downslide. He became angry and paranoid. And when Papa's not happy, ain't nobody happy (to paraphrase).

Anne was executed in May of the same year and King Grouch became less and less active, although he found himself a new sweetheart in Jane Seymour. After her untimely death, Henry mourned by sitting around on his rump and eating massive quantities of food, but refusing to balance out his caloric intake with physical activity. His unhealthy change in size was under way.

In 1539, at age forty-eight, shortly before he married Anne of Cleves, Henry was wearing armor with a waistline of fifty-one inches! And he just kept growing. But we have to remember that the gross and tyrannical Henry that often comes to mind was, for the most part, a later-in-life version of the monarch who started out quite pleasant—appearance- and personality-wise.

Much of the king's drama and appeal (depending on your view) was his all-consuming desire for a son. Since his father's victory at Bosworth Field was not

necessarily the be-all and end-all in terms of job security, Henry VIII's claim to the throne wouldn't be airtight until he had at least a few legitimate sons lined up to take his place when the time rolled around.

He called it quits with Catherine of Aragon, had Anne Boleyn cut down to size, finally rejoiced about the fruit of Jane Seymour's womb, and probably just gave up with the rest of them, deep down inside.

But here's the kicker: he already had a son. A legitimate one? No, of course not. But there was no worry about whether he could produce sons because of a certain Elizabeth "Bessie" Blount, euphemistically referred to as "the king's pastime" among the members of his privy chamber. A gorgeous maid of honor to Catherine of Aragon, she carried on with the king for eight years of his first marriage, and gave birth to his first son in 1519.

The boy's name was Henry, fittingly, and we see him referred to as Henry Fitzroy. Let's check out the origin of that name: Fitz is from the French *fils* (pronounced *feese*), which means "son." Roy is from the French *roi* (pronounced something like *rwah* but it's a tough one if you aren't a native French speaker), which means "king." So Fitzroy is actually "son of the king." Well, bastard son of the king, to be exact.

The Massive Monarch did indeed acknowledge him as an illegitimate son all during the boy's lifetime and gave him fancy-shmancy titles like Duke of Richmond and Earl of Nottingham. By bestowing these titles, it was as if the king had constructed a lighted billboard proclaiming that his wife, the queen, was barren, and that this was as good as it was going to get. This bastard son died (most likely of tuberculosis) at age seventeen, a few months after Anne Boleyn's execution, and is buried in the Howard family tombs at St. Michael's in Framlingham, Suffolk.

THOMAS 101 – SOME KEY TOMS IN HENRY VIII'S REIGN

Doesn't it seem like every other male of this period was named Thomas? A common name for sure, and the moniker used by many a man in Henry VIII's story:

Thomas Wolsey was an incredibly smart, handsome, and hard-working man who found power to be ambrosial, loved pomp and finery, and reveled in his palaces of Whitehall and Hampton Court. He started out in Henry Senior's court as royal chaplain and was given increasingly important positions under Henry Junior. In the early 1520s, he was the wealthiest man in the land, moreso even than the monarch himself. Wolsey made daily visits to the hoi polloi at Westminster Hall, albeit while holding a vinegar-filled orange beneath his nostrils to avoid any olfactory surprises. Wolsey was eventually made a cardinal, though the bishop of Winchester, Richard Fox, complained about having to "deal with a cardinal who is not a cardinal but a king." His elevated status was all well and good when Henry VIII was happy to be an old-school Catholic. But when the Church wouldn't let him sweep his first marriage under the rug, the cardinal became inconvenient. He failed to convince

the pope that Henry and Catherine of Aragon's marriage was invalid due to a loophole, so he couldn't support an outright divorce. Henry pitched a fit and sent him to be imprisoned in London, but Wolsey died on the way after a bout with raging dysentery. Zing!

Thomas Cromwell came from a working-class family with an alcoholic father, and became a member of Parliament as well as Henry VIII's charming right-hand man, secretary, lord privy seal, all that good stuff. Adept at laying on flattery with a trowel, he urged Henry to declare himself head of the new church, which swelled the king's ego even more than it already was. Regardless of how he felt about Anne Boleyn personally, his focus had to be on what the *king* wanted. And the king wanted her *gone*. So Cromwell expedited the break from Anne Boleyn, and ensured that no one could reach Henry for comment, not even Anne's bishops (whom she so desperately wished would defend her as she waited in the Tower shortly before her execution).

He expedited the break from Rome as well, working tirelessly to promote the new religion. After Jane Seymour died, Thomas quickly arranged for a union with Anne of Cleves to gain the Germans' support for the Reformation. Too quickly, apparently, since the king wasn't attracted to Fräulein Cleves, or instead may have been secretly insulted by her failure to fawn all over a bloated and icky monarch. Henry had Cromwell executed and then tortured himself with regret over it for the rest of his life.

Thomas More was a leader in the humanist movement and author of the classic work *Utopia*. He'd set his sights on becoming a monk but couldn't commit to celibacy. More was very close to Henry VIII, who made him his secretary and held his opinions in high esteem. But when one of those opinions was that the king wasn't in charge of the Church, but rather the pope was, More's head rolled onto the scaffold. Because, you see, for Henry, it was a no-brainer: you were either with him (you lived) or against him (you died). For Thomas More, the outcome was clear and there was no decision-making involved for the king. More was canonized as a Catholic saint four hundred years later.

Thomas Cranmer was a leader during the Reformation, when the refreshing new religion came to the shores of England and hit the ground running, starting at the Tudor court. Cranmer was the Archbishop of Canterbury, and a boon to both Henry VIII and his son Edward VI when it came to establishing and promoting Church of England doctrine. Because Henry drifted between the tenets of Catholicism and the new faith, Cranmer kept certain beliefs to himself (such as his anti-transubstantiation view that Christ should be "eaten with the heart"). His successes while playing on Henry's and Edward's teams did him no good when Mary I, a devout Catholic, came to the throne, and he went up in flames.

Thomas Seymour was the brother of Jane Seymour, Henry's third wife, and Edward Seymour, lord protector of England during young Edward VI's reign. Thomas had a reputation as a dashing ladies' man, not diminished by his marriage to Henry's widow, Catherine Parr. Some of his more cringeworthy moments included flirting shamelessly with his stepdaughter, Princess Elizabeth, and being caught outside Edward VI's chambers one night with a pistol. As can be guessed, he was subsequently executed for treason.

Thomas Howard, uncle to Anne Boleyn and Katherine Howard (as well as head of the I Hate Thomas Cranmer club), was born into a noble family and even married a daughter of Edward IV. He became the third duke of Norfolk while Henry VIII was king, but years later was imprisoned for treason after the situation with Henry's fifth wife didn't work out and it seemed to be his fault. He stuck around in prison until Mary I released him.

CATHERINE of ARAGON

DIVORCED
Born: December 16, 1485
Died: January 7, 1536
Married to King Henry
1509 to 1533

ANNE BOLEYN

BEHEADED
Born: 1501?
Died: May 19, 1536
Married to King Henry
1533 to 1536

JANE SEYMOUR

DIED
Born: 1508 or 1509
Died: October 24, 1537
Married to King Henry
1536 to 1537

ANNE of CLEVES

DIVORCED
Born: September 22, 1515
Died: July 16, 1557
Married to King Henry
Jan. 1540 to July 1540

KATHERINE HOWARD

BEHEADED
Born: 1521?
Died: February 13, 1542
Married to King Henry
1540 to 1542

CATHERINE PARR

SURVIVED
Born: 1512?
Died: September 5, 1548
Married to King Henry
1543 to 1547

3

The Wives: Henry's Half Dozen

For better or worse, Henry VIII is often defined at different points of his reign by his wives, so let's start at the very beginning.

WIFE #1: CATHERINE OF ARAGON

Though she was the daughter of King Ferdinand of Aragon, Princess Catherine's reign was not to be in Spain. At the ripe old age of three, she was betrothed to marry the future Henry VIII's older brother, Arthur, who was the heir to the English throne at the time. This was just fine with his younger brother Henry, who was happy to be the Tall, Handsome, Athletic, and Musical One. His family and the royal family of Spain decided to get together by way of their children, so King Ferdinand sent his lovely and vivacious daughter Catherine over in a boat with a huge entourage. She became Arthur's wife when she was a lovely and plump teenager, a gracious and popular princess with wide blue eyes and long auburn hair, and unusually well-read.

After their marriage in November of 1501, the couple was enormously popular. The sixteen-year-old princess of Wales won the people over with her beauty and grace, much like a girl named Diana Spencer did back in 1981 when she married Prince Charles. And then Arthur died, possibly of sweating sickness, just five months after the wedding. Since England and Spain wanted to keep the positive relationship that the marriage had brought, it was decided that Catherine should marry her late husband's brother, Henry.

The only problem was that Henry was just eleven years old! So Catherine waited. And waited. And waited. In a strange land, away from her family. Seven years later, Henry was thrilled to marry his brother's widow at Greenwich Palace (also the site of his wedding to Anne of Cleves, and where he and both of his daughters were born). He stayed married to her for over twenty years before he became Henry VIII the Fickle, Beheading, Power-Mad Monarch.

HE SAID, SHE SAID

Whether Prince Arthur and Catherine of Aragon ever consummated their marriage is a major point of debate in Tudor history. This little matter became a deciding factor for two crucial events of the sixteenth century: Catherine's marriage to Arthur's brother, Henry, and the validity of her marriage to Henry when he planned to tie the knot with Anne Boleyn.

To start off, let's look at how she came to be married to Henry VIII: After Prince Arthur died, Henry VII wasn't keen to simply ship his daughter-in-law

back to Spain. Her father had promised to hand over quite a wad of cash as her dowry, but hadn't followed through. Instead of waiving the bill, Henry Senior planned to pocket the money once he was finally paid, and simply matched her up with his next available son, the tall and handsome Henry Junior.

This next part is important: *She was able to marry Prince Henry only because she swore to the pope that her marriage to The Other Tudor Boy was never consummated*. For the church, this meant that Arthur and Catherine weren't actually married to begin with, and she was free to marry the spare without being seen as an adulteress or trollop of some sort.

Henry VIII and Catherine of Aragon actually spent the early years of their union as an adorable and happy couple. Catherine was a hands-on queen who fancied herself as the unofficial Spanish ambassador to her husband's court. And when England battled Scotland on Flodden Field (eventually killing James IV), it was she who'd led the army north, after having crafted their banners and badges. Catherine consistently lent an air of majesty and professionalism to her role, which reflected well on her king, in turn. Self-control was her modus operandi, emblematic of the Spanish at that time.

Fast-forward a few decades into the marriage and the ginger-haired king still had no legitimate boys to carry on the family business, so he figured he'd just divorce Catherine and remarry. The deeply religious king looked to the Bible to guide his decision and found his aha moment in Leviticus 20:21, which states that a man who marries his brother's wife will be childless (and for Henry, "childless" and "no sons" were practically synonymous). Henry believed that God was punishing him for having married his brother's wife. However, Catherine continued to deny that she and Arthur ever had intimate relations, even though onlookers described them as a fun and loving couple for the short time they were married. Even Arthur's servants had claimed that he called for wine on the morning after his wedding, adding that (TMI alert!) he had "been in Spain, and it was thirsty work." In retrospect, because we know he may have died of tuberculosis, we might also speculate that he could have suffered from a low sex drive as a result of the disease, a bust for his marital relations if not for his storytelling ability.

Was the prince trying to save face with his peers, avoiding the embarrassment of admitting he didn't know his new bride intimately? Or did the Spanish infanta with the spotless reputation lie? Why wouldn't a young couple who seemed to be happy and in love consummate their marriage? Do we believe what he said? Or what she said?

Decades later, while Henry worked on a way to finally live happily ever after with his newest obsession (see Wife #2), he notified his wife that it was to be over between them. However, Catherine wasn't going down like that, and continued to sit alongside him in public, affecting happiness.

Frustrated, he finally banished her from court. She'd already been denied the company of their daughter, Mary, for years and wasn't even allowed a visit before she succumbed to what was likely a cancerous tumor. Catherine, the toast of the English court way back when, was only the first of Henry's many matrimonial casualties. After her death, the king and his latest gal, Anne Boleyn, decked themselves out in yellow. The color signified joy or mourning, depending on whom you ask. The shade they wore was most likely *schadenfreude*—a bad color on anyone.

THE BREAK WITH ROME

Our young Henry VIII was considered a devout Catholic, attending Mass three times a day, being buddy-buddy with the pope, and strongly defending the idea of transubstantiation (the changing of the bread and wine into the body and blood of Christ).

Similarly, the lives of other Tudor-era folk revolved around God—His laws, judgment, rewards, and punishment. All sixteenth-century debate came down to religion at some point in the proceeding, and early in that era, Christians in England were Catholic. Meanwhile, back in Germany in 1526, a priest named Martin Luther was busy organizing his new church after rejecting the Catholic Church, which was fraught with corruption at that time. It had been spiraling out of control in a downward direction, not helped by the fact that the clergy had become such poor examples by carrying weapons, lazing about in taverns, and keeping a sloppy appearance. Luther's work sparked the Reformation, and Christianity was then split in two: Catholics and, eventually, Protestants

He was especially riled up about pay-to-pray indulgences, the implication from some high-profile

Catholics that prayer was all that stood between Purgatory and Heaven, and that money could buy such prayer. His doctrines were banned and burned, but continued to be smuggled into England. The German lashed out at Henry VIII's Defense of the Sacraments and dubbed the king a "damnable and rotten worm." Henry slammed Luther as a "wolf of Hell." Sticks and stones, gentlemen!

Around this time, thirty-five-year-old Henry was frustrated that Catherine had failed to produce a male heir who could live past infancy. On New Year's Day back in 1511, the queen had given birth to a boy who was welcomed with trumpet blasts, jousts, fires, and "a pageant devised like a mountain, glistening by night as though it had been all gold and set with stones." All for naught: the child died during the following month.

Henry and Catherine's only surviving child was little Princess Mary. They'd been married for nearly twenty years, and to what end? One measly daughter? He ranted and raved and stomped his feet when the pope wouldn't let him pretend that his marriage didn't exist so he could get on with a new one. But in the end he declared himself the head of the brand-new Church of England. And isn't that convenient? He dumped Catherine and married a certain lady of the court named Anne Boleyn, as if she'd had "can produce male babies" stamped on her forehead. He embraced blossoming Reformist ideals such as married priests, no confession, and no transubstantiation.

Like a petulant child, he destroyed a ton of monasteries in England and cut off the heads of important

Catholics in the country. That oughta teach 'em! But it didn't help Queen Anne give birth to any healthy boys, nor did it keep his next wife, Jane Seymour, alive long enough to have more than one male heir. He couldn't even stomach staying in the same room with Anne of Cleves (Wife #4), let alone touch her with a ten-foot pole.

Then in 1539 (right between Wives 4 and 5), Henry convinced Parliament to pass the Act of Six Articles, which basically said:

- Transubstantiation is A-OK once again.
- Communion is to be bread only, not wine.
- Priests can't be married.
- Payment for get-out-of-purgatory prayer is fine.
- Widows can't remarry.
- Confession must be made to a priest.
- Sound familiar?

For several decades after his death, Henry's Catholic daughter Mary and his Protestant-friendly daughter Elizabeth duked it out, keeping the country divided by religion. But for all intents and purposes, Henry, in his heart, was still a Catholic.

WIFE #2: ANNE BOLEYN

History has painted Henry's second wife as a scheming, opportunistic witch (to put it mildly). It doesn't help that she was preceded by Wife #1, the well-loved Catherine of Aragon, and followed by seemingly angelic Wife #3, Jane Seymour. Pop culture likes to

suggest that Anne practically batted her eyelashes at the married king, enticed him to leave his wife for a woman who could surely give him a son, and convinced him to abandon his beloved Catholic church for a newfangled religion that would ensure he answered to no one but God.

Let's back up for a minute. Anne wasn't European royalty but she wasn't Jane-Doe-off-the-street either. Her father, Thomas, was a soldier for the original Tudor monarch, Henry VII, and Henry VIII made Papa Boleyn the ambassador to France. When Anne's father moved her and her siblings back to England, the girls became ladies-in-waiting to the queen, Catherine of Aragon.

The first outward sign that the king had the hots for Anne Boleyn was on Shrove Tuesday in 1526. He wore a costume with a flaming heart and the words "Declare I dare not," as subtle as a sledgehammer, and a birdbrained thing to do considering he already had a loving queen who was adored by the people. (Conversely, Anne was never a crowd-pleaser. When he took her to France, his own sister, that country's queen, snubbed them and wouldn't see them across the Channel. And none of his relatives showed up for her coronation.)

When these verboten urges began to smolder, Henry and Catherine had been married for sixteen male-heir-free years. Mary Boleyn, Anne's sister, was awfully pretty, and Henry couldn't resist getting involved with her for several years. Interestingly enough, Thomas Boleyn was then given a promotion in the king's court, though Henry bored of Mary quickly and no longer paid her any attention. Easy come, easy go.

Mary was a famous beauty, but Anne had brains as well as an unusual look to her. Long-necked and flat-chested with bewitching dark eyes and a big mouth (literally as well as figuratively), she appeared in marked contrast to the ideal woman of the time, which was a light-haired and light-eyed lass with rosebud lips.

She was unique in appearance, literate, and witty . . . the king was intrigued. Remember that at this time Henry was not only tall, fit, handsome, athletic, and a talented musician, he was also, you know, the king. Power can be very attractive, as can be womanly charm and intelligence. Henry VIII and Anne Boleyn certainly made quite the dynamic duo!

As more time passed in her premarital relationship with Henry, her sassiness snowballed. Soon, she was insulting the king's men and mouthing off indiscriminately.

Still, she was a smart cookie, and while their relationship continued to sizzle, she told him that it couldn't get too far while he was married. The king's first attempt to have his first marriage annulled was in the spring of 1527, but he wouldn't have a second wife until over five hot-and-bothered years later.

Considering Anne Boleyn's personality, upbringing, and family, is it any surprise that Anne and Henry got together? Or that, after the king began to show an interest in Anne, Thomas Boleyn helped push the pope toward a divorce for Henry and Catherine? And is it any surprise that Thomas then got another promotion?

It's whom you know, isn't it? Anne was able to marry the most powerful man in the land largely because of her father's connections within the Tudor dynasty. Thomas rose in the ranks because of her flirtation and then marriage to Henry. Was Anne an insolent homewrecker? Or was she a political pawn for daddy-dearest's ambition?

In January 1533, Anne and the smitten monarch were married in a secret ceremony in his private chapel at Whitehall Palace. Only a handful of people were present, and they had to promise to stay mum about the newlyweds.

Speaking of mum, Anne was already a few months pregnant with the future Elizabeth I at the time. Apparently, Anne and Henry were first secretly married the previous November. Bam! She'd gotten pregnant almost immediately.

Either way, their union wasn't considered valid until Henry's marriage to the estranged Catherine of Aragon was officially kaput in May. The new king and queen's entwined initials became their monogram, and as could be expected, the jokes wrote themselves since these initials together spelled HA. The monogram was engraved here, there, and everywhere, posing a challenge after Anne's downfall when evidence of her queenship needed to be erased. Most of them were destroyed eventually, but a few forgotten ones remain, such as that in the ceiling of the gatehouse at Hampton Court Palace.

When newlywed Anne Boleyn gave birth, the child turned out to be healthy, adorable, and ... a girl. Little Elizabeth wasn't of the desired sex, but at least she

gained the titles of princess and heir, which Catherine of Aragon's little girl was then denied. (That was a moot point, since the teenager kept using her title anyway.) The pro-Princess-Mary faction reported that Anne, while under the guise of improving relations between king and daughter, tried to force teenaged Mary to admit that her parents' marriage was an unlawful sham, embarrassing the girl at fancy meals in her own home.

Wife #2 went on to lose two babies, the final one being a boy. This was so not turning out as Henry had planned, and now his attentions had turned to one of the queen's ladies-in-waiting, Jane Seymour. As the story will prove, Hell hath no fury like a jilted Anne Boleyn.

Her quick wit and fiery nature, which at first attracted the king, likely began to grate on his nerves. What good was a queen if she couldn't give him a surviving son? Her reproductive challenges, her clashes with Thomas Cromwell regarding foreign policy, and her offhanded but awkward comments to men such as court musician Mark Smeaton all contributed to her swift downfall in the spring of 1536.

Interestingly, treason was one thing she'd actually committed, although likely not through physical frivolity. While speaking with Henry Norris at an earlier time, she uttered the sentiment, "If anything happens to the king, you would look to have me." Quite a faux pas, as speculating on the monarch's death was a treasonous activity, and yet another strike against her during these bloody days. It's worth noting, however, that while modern accounts of her undoing claim

otherwise, there's no mention of the word "witch-craft" in the records of the proceedings against her.

Four unfortunate men went on trial at Westminster Hall and were found guilty of having their trousers around their ankles in the company of the queen. They were: Henry Norris, the aforementioned Groom of the Stool and Chief Gentleman of the Privy Chamber; William Brererton, Groom of the Privy Chamber; Francis Weston, a young lad who'd been Henry's favorite page in the past; and Mark Smeaton, the aforementioned court musician.

Were they actually guilty? Most likely not. But they were sentenced to be executed regardless. They'd be dragged individually by a horse-drawn cart to a scaffold on Tower Hill where they'd be hanged—almost. The executioner would take them down just before the rope actually did them in, only to chop off their naughty bits and then hack them into quarters. Fortunately, Good King Hal commuted all their sentences to a simple beheading.

The fifth to be accused was Anne's own brother, George, who only became wrapped up in this mess when his wife, who was understandably miffed about some previous extramarital dalliances of his, named him as another notch on the queen's bedpost. The aristocratic sibling team of Anne and George were given the privilege of a separate trial due to their social standing, and for security reasons. They were charged, falsely, with incest, and would die for it. Although his execution was on the private Tower Green, another reward for his elevated station, George met the ax like the other wrongly accused men. But Anne was

afforded the dignity of being beheaded by The Best: a master swordsman sent from France. *Merci!*

Henry's second queen was not about to throw on any old thing for the last morning of her life. Her choices were deliberate, if deliciously fashionable as well. To start with, Anne wore a heavy black damask robe for her "small, private" audience of about a thousand people. The damask she wore would have been a thick fabric made of silk, linen, or wool and embroidered with a shiny satin pattern over top.

The robe was trimmed in ermine, that white fur (sometimes with little black spots) so often seen in frou-frou portraits of nobility. The ermine is a type of weasel and a symbol of royalty. Anne certainly broke out the ermine to drive home the point that she was still the queen, doggone it.

Underneath the weasel-trimmed threads, Anne wore a rich red petticoat. Red symbolized martyrdom, so she was making a crystal-clear statement about her innocence. Beneath a gable hood, she wore a netted coif to keep her locks from getting in the swordsman's way, because no one wants to hit a speed bump during a beheading.

Witnesses say she strutted to the scaffold with an air of aplomb. Well why not, in those clothes? She kneeled and her ladies removed her headdress and applied a blindfold. While praying aloud for Christ to take her soul, Anne was distracted by the executioner's call for his sword. Her head turned, the man whipped the weapon from its hiding place in the straw on the scaffold, and that was that.

Although it was said she looked absolutely wiped out (lack of sleep can do that) and kept checking over her shoulder (perhaps for a last-minute reprieve?), she is said to have been the picture of composure and strength. Onlookers described Anne as having "a devilish walk" and "never look[ing] more beautiful," "full of much joy and pleasure." Her final speech was heartfelt yet professional.

And because the executioner had hidden his sword in the straw and distracted Anne with the infamous "Hey, what's that over there?" trick, she never saw it coming. Her Grace was poised to the end.

CATHOLIC VERSUS REFORMIST

The terms Catholic and Protestant (or to be more accurate for the time of Henry VIII's reign, Reformist) can't be applied to the Tudor period as they are applied today. Just as political parties have evolved over decades and centuries to be quite different from their roots, so have these two branches of Christianity. But let's think about how this exciting yet tumultuous time in religious history may have looked to both sides.

On the one hand, we have the Reformers (a term first coined in this context by Thomas Cranmer in the spring of 1536). These are the folks who embraced the "alternative" wave that was sweeping mainland Europe and evolved into what we know now as Protestantism. In the Tudor cast of characters, this includes Anne Boleyn (to an extent), Edward VI, Lady Jane Grey, and, eventually, Catherine Parr. They'd had it with the greedy and controlling ways of influential sixteenth-century Catholics, and seemed to be moved by the breath of fresh air that came with the Reformation. It was a great time to cast off the oppressive chains of Rome and introduce the people to what Christ really wanted for his people. Henry was also tired of being the Vatican's puppet. It was a time to declare himself head of his country's church instead of being controlled from way over yonder.

On the other hand, we have the Catholics, who included Catherine of Aragon and Mary I. Like most people in Tudor England, they grew up with Catholicism. It was ingrained in their psyche and was the reason for all the traditions they took part in during the year. For devout Catholics, it was an important part of their soul.

Henry died with a firm grip on Catholicism. He denounced the Church and even got himself excommunicated, but it seems his flirtation with the Reformation had these goals in mind: divorce Catherine of Aragon, get on with legitimately siring a son, and get out from under Rome's control. As for Elizabeth I, she didn't advertise her personal religious convictions but applied her mastery of politics to keep England itself Protestant and bring stability to the nation.

Because England, in the end, embraced Protestantism, the historical view of the Catholic Tudors tends to be that they were "stubborn," "bitter," "fanatical," and so forth. Make no mistake: Mary I was certainly fanatical. But so was Edward VI. And had Lady Jane Grey lived, she may have been a match for their theological passion. Is it fair to dismiss the attachment that Mary, Catherine of Aragon, et al had to Catholicism simply because others embraced the new kid on the blessed block?

Given the climate of the Church at the time, it's understandable how the disgruntled (or those who just never "felt" Catholicism in their hearts) would be eager to give Rome the boot and explore the fresher path to Christ that Martin Luther and other Protestant pioneers offered. However, nearly 1500 years of Catholicism preceded the Reformation, and for plenty of people it was their soul's true calling.

Sure, the leaders of Tudor England had political motives tied to their stance on the country's religion. But whether a monarch wanted to keep England Catholic or make it Protestant, the personal convictions in each ruler's heart should be respected. In short, the religious beliefs of these monarchs were as follows:

- Henry VIII—Whatever suited him, and he wasn't secretive about it.
- Catherine of Aragon—Unapologetically Catholic.
- Mary I—See above, plus a dash of extremism.
- Anne Boleyn—Reformation-curious but asked for confession and the sacrament before her execution.
- Catherine Parr—Practiced Catholicism with an open mind but walked that fence very carefully and later took to the new religion.
- Edward VI—Flag-waving teen Protestant.
- Lady Jane Grey—Protestant poster child.
- Elizabeth I—Kept her beliefs to herself.

In such a volatile time, discussing your religious beliefs was tricky, if not fatal.

Was it more important to be true to faith, putting aside earthly happenings for a reward after death and to keep your soul at peace? Or to zip it, lock it, and put it in your pocket for the sake of running the country or dealing with those who did?

By trumpeting her beliefs and sticking to them, was Catherine of Aragon "stubborn" or "brave"? By keeping hers nebulous, was Elizabeth I "a noncommittal coward" or "smart"?

WIFE #3: JANE SEYMOUR

Although Henry VIII had already fathered a son with his mistress, Bessie Blount, he was still on a quest for a bouncing baby boy who wasn't a bastard. Enter Jane Seymour, lady-in-waiting to Anne Boleyn and sister to Thomas and Edward Seymour. Henry and Jane's flirtation began at some time during his marriage to Anne, when he sent her letters and other goodies. She responded by going on about her honor and how she absolutely would not lose it. Because there was, apparently, nothing Henry loved more than forbidden fruit, this reeled him right in. They were wed just eleven days after Anne's execution because time was ticking for that produce-an-heir situation. Besides, the sooner the last queen was forgotten, the better.

Plain Jane's appeal is a bit of a mystery, but she probably scored big points for appearing to be a 180-degree turn from Anne Boleyn. Mousy, obedient, practically transparent in the complexion depart-

ment, and with no talent to speak of, she portrayed herself as a lover, not a fighter. Her gentle push toward a Henry-Princess Mary reconciliation was another point for her peacemaker image, although it was probably also a product of her family's Catholic bent.

This inclination, however, couldn't have been too much of a bonus, considering that her short time as queen coincided with the tragic events of the Pilgrimage of Grace, when the northern Catholics were mobilizing against their king in the wake of the Dissolution of the Monasteries. (Didn't these people know that Henry had recently fallen from his horse in a dreadful jousting accident and was starting to lose his marbles because of it?) Jane wasn't too proud to beg on her knees for her husband to restore these houses of God he'd wiped out. But that wasn't going to happen, and Henry's reaction ensured that her histrionics wouldn't happen again, either. Lesson learned.

Nonetheless, after two marriages with Spanish and French sensibilities, respectively, Henry relished the fact that Jane was English to the tips of her toes. Who better, finally, to serve as queen of his country and mother to his heir? When the couple had been married for a bit over a year, Jane gave birth to that long-awaited follow-up act, Prince Edward. But just two weeks later, she lay dead.

Puerperal fever, caused by a uterine infection, usually takes the blame. In Jane's day, and through the nineteenth century, it was common for new mothers to die in this way. For one thing, there were no antibiotics to treat the infection. And it was much easier to become infected in the first place because there were no signs advising that "All employees must wash hands before delivering each baby" where doctors worked back then. Physicians didn't wash their instruments either, let alone sterilize them. It's a wonder new moms survived at all.

Had Jane lived, would the king's eye have roved once again? Would her brothers' calculating personalities eventually come through in her as well, tarnishing her image of one "bound to obey and serve," her queenly motto? Because tragedy closed the door on Jane Seymour's story prematurely, such speculation is simply a non-issue. What remained was her greatest accomplishment: a legitimate son and heir for Henry VIII.

WIFE #4: ANNE OF CLEVES

"A Flanders mare, not a Venus." Poor Anne of Cleves bears the reputation of being Henry's ugly wife. The king had seen the portrait that Hans Holbein the Younger had painted of the German noblewoman and thought it quite nice, but he wasn't nearly so taken in person. However, it wasn't Henry but rather the seventeenth-century bishop Gilbert Burnet who is credited with that infamous sentiment, misinterpreted as an equine slam against the king's newest lady by Henry himself.

By the time Wife #4 was on deck, the king needed another marriage for several reasons, and the birth of an heir was not the least of them. But he also needed a new Mrs. to brighten up the mood of the court, which

was still cloaked in the shadow of Jane Seymour's untimely demise. Potential mates included Marie de Guise (future mother to Mary Queen of Scots), as well as Marguerite de Valois, Anne of Lorraine, and Christina of Milan, who was rumored to have made the brassy comment that she'd consider the match only if she possessed one head to spare.

A pairing with the lady from Düsseldorf was Thomas Cromwell's brainchild and had political motivations. Although Anne's brother, the duke of Cleves, wasn't Lutheran himself, he had strong ties to the leader of the Protestant movement in Germany, John Frederick I. Naturally, this ticked the important "politics and religion" box for any potential queen of Henry's at that moment. When the king began to have second thoughts, he realized that a change of plans might drive the duke into the hands of his religious rivals, Charles V (the Holy Roman Emperor and king of Spain) and Francis I (king of, naturally, France). His lamentation? "Now it is too far gone, wherefore I am sorry." That being said, sorry doesn't butter the biscuit, and that's how Anne of Cleves became a part of this saga.

Her education was dull, and her artistic skills were similarly limited. While she reveled in needlework, she could neither sing nor play any musical instruments (she reportedly had a tin ear), likely a huge letdown for a king of immense culture who adored his song and dance.

Anne of Cleves was entirely foreign to Henry; it mattered not that she descended from strong English royal stock in the form of Edward I and Eleanor of

Castille. She lacked the confident majesty of Catherine of Aragon, the playful zest of Anne Boleyn, and the pure Englishness and obedience of Jane Seymour. This man and woman were as different as chalk and cheese.

Then there was the infamous issue of appearance. Contemporary sources described Jane Seymour's successor as superior to beauties of her time, right down to the charming dimples in her cheeks and on her chin. But even if a negative spin on Anne of Cleves' physical attributes had been exaggerated, the nearly-fifty-year-old monarch was no prize himself by that time. He'd gone from a fit, handsome, charming young guy who could joust and compose musical pieces with the best of them to a fat old guy with an oozing leg sore and a bad case of oppositional defiant disorder.

He was, however, still a bit of a practical joker, which proved disastrous for his first meeting with Anne. Her arrival had been significantly delayed due to weather conditions and geographic technicalities, and by then the impatient king was at the end of his rope. When she was finally in his sights as she watched (and was apparently bored to bits by) her own welcoming festivities, the king disguised himself as a messenger who was bestowing gifts upon the newcomer. This wasn't a woman who played games, so she blew him off and went back to the ennui-inducing show before her. Henry dashed out and changed into his regal garments, and swept back in to reveal his true identity to the perplexed guest. And because first impressions are lasting impressions, this match was ultimately doomed.

As months of this marriage wore on, Henry became consumed not only with disappointment in her looks but also with the paranoid thought that her purity wasn't as had been advertised to him, due to "the feel of her belly and her breasts." The newlyweds never consummated their marriage, which was just as well because the two were utterly incompatible as romantic partners. Perhaps Anne 2.0 didn't gush all over the king as he was used to? Perhaps she wounded his pride a bit? They say flattery gets you everywhere, but in this case failure to fawn gets you zero physical contact and a quick annulment. Six months after their wedding at Greenwich Palace, Henry declared that Anne would be henceforth known as his "beloved sister" and gifted her with lovely palaces as part of their divorce settlement. Not too shabby! He was then on to Wife #5.

WIFE #5: KATHERINE HOWARD

By the time the teenaged Katherine Howard married Henry, he'd gone from a hot, athletic, charming young prince to . . . well, one hot fifty-one-year-old mess. His newest queen was a tiny street-smart temptress decked out in French fashions, the anti-Anne-of-Cleves.

Although Katherine fulfilled her wifely duties in the bed-chamber and was savvy at stroking the king's ego, she likely had an affair as well, at least emotional if not also physical. Her partner in crime was the young and aesthetically pleasing gentleman of Henry's privy chamber, Thomas Culpeper. Big mistake.

(And boyfriends from her pre-queen days only added to her dirty laundry.)

When the word hit the cobblestone street, she was put under house arrest at Hampton Court. Palace legend claims that she briefly escaped her captors at one point and raced down a Hampton Court hallway to beg the king's mercy, but that the guards caught her and dragged her screaming back to her holding place. She was imprisoned for a few months and then executed in February 1542. After her execution, Henry was a different man and moped around in a state of sadness, sighing as he went. Matrimony-wise, the light at the end of the tunnel was becoming no more than a pinpoint for the aging monarch.

How does Henry's fifth wife fit in among the rest? In modern times, Katherine Howard often has the reputation of having been a young, pretty hussy, and dumb as a box of rocks. But he was infatuated with her right away, the old scamp, and married her in July 1540.

There were loads of activities that summer to celebrate the new girl on the block, who seemed to have already been around the block a few times, though it would take a while for that bit to come to light. Her husband lavished her with sumptuous jewelry—gold chains, brooches, crosses, and even books, all laden with diamonds, rubies, pearls, and other swoon-worthy gems. Young Katherine spent lots of time dancing in fine dresses and savored her new role as queen. Who can blame her? The poor girl came from nothing and could have never imagined a life such as this.

Her father, Edmund, was one of twenty-three children in a noble family. He lost everything, but kept his hand out for, well, a handout. In his final years, he was reduced to an incontinent. His third wife hit him when he'd helplessly wet their bed and humiliated him with taunts that only children did such things.

Motherless Katherine had meanwhile been growing up in the youth home run by her step-grandmother. The girl was poor, uneducated, unrefined, and lost in the shuffle. So when she eventually came to live in palaces and receive horses and jewels and such, she could hardly believe her luck.

Katherine had a joyful disposition as well as a sweet nature. She felt for the prisoners her husband had locked away in the Tower of London, and she even managed to get two of them released. A third prisoner, Margaret Pole, Countess of Salisbury, was not so lucky, though Katherine herself paid for the elderly woman to be warmly and appropriately dressed in her damp, cold cell.

All her dancing and prancing and coquettish ways eventually did her in, as she was accused of adultery and lost that pretty head a year and a half after all those grand wedding celebrations. The wildcard of the six wives wanted to be prepared for the ax and reportedly practiced placing her head on a block brought to her cell in the Tower. On the scaffold the following morning, she spoke about having offended God from an early age and breaking all his commandments. She then prayed for the king and asked for God's mercy before laying her head on a block for the final time. It may have been one of the few things she got right.

WIFE #6: CATHERINE PARR

You might think Henry, near the end of his life, was a fervent anti-Catholic after all the "Great Matter" hoopla and needing to stick it to the pope in order to divorce Catherine of Aragon and marry Anne Boleyn (who, by this time, was four wives ago). On the contrary, Henry was still strongly Catholic in his beliefs and happy to persecute Reformist heretics.

His wife during this period was the twice-widowed Catherine Parr. It's evident by now that hers was a fairly common female name at the time. In fact, her mother named her after Wife #1. A Yorkist descendant, Maud Parr had been lady-in-waiting to Catherine of Aragon during the early years of Henry's reign and thought highly enough of the queen to use the same moniker for her baby daughter. When said daughter was just eleven years old, Maud started searching for the girl's future husband, because Catherine (although descended from the English royals via several routes) had no title and no impressive fortune, two things that could only be hers through marriage.

The last of Henry's wives was a polished and well-educated English woman who was adept at hunting, riding, and playing chess. A fashionista and lover of fine fabrics, she adored the color red, and even padded the seat in her swank lavatory with crimson velvet. Catherine was attractive and made sure to keep herself desirable for her new husband, luxuriating in skin-softening milk baths and outfitting herself in the finest fabrics. On the day following their wedding, she placed an order for perfumes for her bedchamber and

soon added to the enticing atmosphere with heaps of herb sachets. Since the room was above the kitchen, a certain amount of deodorizing couldn't have hurt.

The new couple shared a love of dancing and reading. There's no reason to believe they didn't genuinely enjoy each other's company. Although Henry was immense by then, this wasn't a pity marriage. Henry took those dazzling jewels that had been Katherine Howard's and showered them on her successor. "All that glittered" was a royal girl's best friend, especially if she had an uncompromised neck on which to display them.

Catherine Parr had been Wife #6 for three years when she nearly landed herself in a heap of trouble. She'd held a soft spot for Protestants who were viewed as heretics, probably because she herself subscribed to the new faith but kept it hush-hush from the king. In fact, she had a friend named Anne Askew, who was an enthusiastic preacher of Reformist ideals and ended up taking quite a bit of heat for it, so to speak. When the woman was questioned at length on her beliefs, she passionately denied the concept of transubstantiation and was tossed into the Tower. Racked within an inch of her life, and then having sat on a bare floor for two hours arguing her case, she held her ground and needed to be brought to her fate at the stake by chair, since the torture rendered her near-broken.

Catherine's sympathy for women such as Anne Askew, plus her spirited religious debates with her husband, plus Henry's state of mind (paranoid, angry, and in pain from his oozing leg sore) all added up to his idea to have a warrant drawn up for Catherine's

arrest when the rumor got out that she was trying to bring down the king's religion. Although he signed it, his servant dropped it and it was found by Catherine's own servant. That was close!

The queen was hysterical at the news, perhaps even worrying that she might be the next headless wife of Henry VIII. When he finally had a chat with her about it, she calmly and diplomatically explained that she'd only debated religion with him to distract him from his leg pain, and also to learn more about religion for herself.

Success! He bought it and spared her any repercussions. She kept her mouth shut for the next six months and outlived Henry when his body, likely exhausted from diabetes, finally gave up. (The king's end was private but undignified: He'd already endured months of incessant pain, and his ailing bulk had needed to be moved about by wheeled chairs and pullies.)

Mere months after the king's death, Catherine married yet again. Her next and final husband was none other than her pre-Henry crush, Thomas Seymour, court rogue and one of Jane Seymour's brothers. He'd be described by Princess Elizabeth after his death as "a man of much wit and little judgment," and had a reputation of being beastly and conniving. But Thomas can be slightly redeemed by the facts that he was charismatic, well-traveled, adventurous, a fierce friend, and had a fantastic singing voice and no illegitimate children (if we're into questionable standards).

Despite her new marriage, she was still styled "Kateryn the Quene" and Thomas addressed her as "Your

Highness," so not exactly a union on equal footing. Before long, Thomas and Catherine were expecting a baby, and the mom-to-be herself, though fatigued and morning-sick, outfitted a splendid nursery at Sudeley Castle. But childbirth did Catherine in. Racked with infection and delirium, she only became the "survived" in the famous mnemonic for a short while.

So who was the true survivor? Of Henry's six wives, it was Anne of Cleves who outlived them all.

A FAVORITE WIFE?

With six wives to choose from, perhaps Henry had a favorite. The demure and tactful Jane Seymour usually gets credit for being The One, but that may be taking the easy route. Sure, compared to his previous wife (Anne Boleyn), Jane knew when to keep her trap shut and didn't stir the pot. And her uterus nurtured the elusive Y chromosome with which Henry was obsessed. So by sixteenth-century royal standards, she'd done her job.

And then she dropped dead and really could do no wrong after that. Bowing out at the top of her game was an unwittingly wise move on her part, because history paints her as the Golden Wife as a result. She didn't live long enough to have miscarriages or dreaded baby girls, or enter middle age, or be grossed out by his oozing leg sore or mid-life obesity. In fact, Jane and Henry lie together for eternity in their shared tomb in the floor of St. George's Chapel at Windsor Castle. Also, it's Jane who is depicted as the queen in the 1545 painting "The Family of Henry VIII," which hangs in a Hampton Court Palace hallway. How might Catherine Parr, his final wife, have felt about these apparent snubs? Easy: She didn't take them as snubs. She was fully aware that Jane was given a place of honor to underscore Henry's ideal Tudor family, from which his heir's mother was inseparable.

But let's take a look at Henry's other ladies. Catherine of Aragon was a thorn in his side toward the end of their marriage, for sure, and she only gave him one daughter. But she was a dutiful and loving wife for more than twenty years, not to mention a popular Spanish princess and a pious Catholic. Wife #2, the self-assured Anne Boleyn, was such an effective flirt that the king was convinced she was flirting with others, although it's never been proven. She tapped into his randy side and he surely admired her charisma and intelligence.

After the dearly departed Jane, Anne of Cleves (we're at number 4, now) is often remembered as a bit of a dull dishrag. But the poor girl couldn't speak a lick of English and communication is so important, isn't it? Plus, there was her reputedly disappointing appearance and the high odds that she was repulsed by this sizable mass of conceit and rage. After their divorce, Henry viewed Anne of Cleves as a sister, gave her a lovely settlement, and invited her to court quite a bit. The favorite, no, but not the outcast, either.

In flounces Wife #5, Katherine Howard. Katherine seemed to be low on brain cells but high on the vixen factor. Henry appreciated the coquette angle, certainly, but he craved more than just glossy paintwork. And her rendering him a cuckold didn't help matters. Finally we have Wife #6, Catherine Parr, by whom he may have even felt a bit upstaged, as she was a published author and a strong influence on his kids. Her attractiveness and smarts wrapped up the king's marital history on a high note.

Out of that cast of characters, do you think Henry truly had a favorite? Whom do you think he held most near and dear? Or do you feel that his greatest love the whole time was actually the one he saw in the looking glass?

4

Edward VI:
Here Comes the Son!

Henry VIII waited and waited (and divorced and beheaded) for a legitimate male heir who would live past infancy, and in 1537 he finally got one, thanks to Wife #3, Jane Seymour. The boy ended up dying at age fifteen, from what many historians believe was tuberculosis. His father was a tough act to follow. But what do we know about the boy king?

Named for his great-grandfather (Edward IV, father of Elizabeth of York), Edward VI was only nine years old when he ascended the throne, inheriting the rule of a country whose inflation was out of control. His coronation marked the first time a new monarch was blessed/saddled with the title "Supreme Head of the Church of England." Three crowns were used for the occasion, an allusion to the pope's triple crown and, thus, an "in your face" directed at Rome.

Since he wasn't of legal age, he made no decisions at this time: rather, his protector did it for him. As the only male heir, he was quite shielded from the time he was born. His father, too, had been coddled once he'd moved from first-runner-up position to heir apparent, but that wasn't until he was thirteen years old.

In young Edward's day, children were dying at alarming rates. So, everything he touched—food, clothes, all of it—was micromanaged in an effort to get this kid safely to the throne. Servants practically sterilized his rooms three times each day, and no one accessed the baby prince without his father's express permission.

Though protected and pampered, he had a comparatively enjoyable childhood, with plenty of playmates and playthings. Naturally, he had only the best educational training, and proved to be quite the royal brainiac. His studies were a chocolate box of such goodies as Greek, Latin, French, music, history, and geography. While he'd later have kind words to describe his teacher, Richard Cox, the man who was known as a "great teacher but also a great beater" would whack the heck out of Edward when he couldn't take the kid's stubbornness any longer.

Edward was patient for his age (or anyone's age, for that matter) and loved to listen to long sermons in church. He was also fussy and could be a bit of a buzzkill. When his sister Mary was enjoying her twenties and dancing the day away, he warned her that all that frivolous dancing would damage her reputation. Of course, that dancing wouldn't put nearly as large a dent in her reputation as the subsequent Marian Burnings would, but let's not get ahead of ourselves. The boy also forbade his sister from hearing Mass, citing that she was his subject and answered to him. Although religion drove a wedge between them in time, young Edward was quite close to Mary. She and their half-sister, Elizabeth, doted on the boy and he adored them in return.

The little king was a reliable pen pal for his stepmother, Catherine Parr, although as he grew older he often took the opportunity to comment patronizingly on her Latin. For the bright and literate former queen, that surely got old pretty quickly.

However, he didn't exactly have the "powerful" image down pat, as his father did. All the robes and feathers and codpieces in the world would not have changed the fact that Edward was a scrawny scrap o'nothing with one shoulder noticeably higher than the other. He feared Henry and, sadly, became rattled by paternal visits.

Although England was still officially Catholic when he was born, the young king became a fanatical Protestant with the help of his protectors and teachers. He would yap on and on to others about Catholic heretics and fire and brimstone. He could have come off as quite a bore except that he was the king and might not mind cutting you down to size if you outwardly challenged his views on the pope. Under Edward's rule, churches were stripped of all ornamentation, and missing Sunday church services meant six months in the slammer (the *first* time). And, of course, transubstantiation wasn't up for discussion.

For all intents and purposes, the true rulers during Edward VI's reign were John Dudley, Duke of Northumberland, and the boy's uncle and protector, Edward Seymour, Duke of Somerset. The elder Seymour brother (whose siblings were Wife #3 and Thomas, widower of Catherine Parr) pushed Protestantism forcefully. The massive amount of rebels in the north didn't care for that, and a few years later, he was executed. His young majesty described the event succinctly in his diary: "The Duke of Somerset had his head cut off on Tower Hill." And that was all.

Young Edward only sat on the throne for six years. The intended savior of the post-Henry dynasty was smacked down by measles, and although his illness was a short one, it may have contributed to his death.

The spotty sickness is thought to suppress the body's natural immunity to tuberculosis, and he would have only needed to be exposed to the pulmonary disease briefly after having had measles. His swift downward spiral came at the start of 1553 and gained momentum with each passing month, during which time his half-sister Mary (and indirect successor) prayed for him fervently. Scattered fevers and fits of coughing gave way to a major drop in weight and some amazing Technicolor vomit: yellow, green, black, and pink.

By late May, the boy king's demise was a done deal. Edward had grown up draped in the most gorgeous fabrics and in the most sumptuous settings, but now all vanity took a back seat. He was coughing up a black carbon-like substance that stunk to the high heavens and sank when placed in a basin of water. His hair and nails were falling out, and his skin was turning blue. He was wasting away and yet blew up like a balloon. The "medicine" he was given was a concoction of raisins, dates, turnips, celery, pork, fennel, and spearmint syrup.

He whispered his last prayer on a July evening in 1553, while a fierce thunderstorm raged outside his windows and red hailstones pelted the earth.

By six o'clock he was dead and the Lady Jane Grey saga began. When Edward's physicians performed his autopsy, they found huge black pits in his lungs, smelly with decay. The findings are consistent with death from TB, though at the time many thought (from his skin color and swellings) that he had been poisoned. Tuberculosis is the likely cause, but it's never been determined exactly what finished off that long-awaited, celebrated heir.

5

Lady Jane Grey: Blink and You'll Miss Her

Next came a Grey area in the succession. Literally. In 1553, Henry VIII's beloved son had been reduced, sadly, to a nearly bald, coughing, vomiting, bloated mass of ulcers. Who would take over, once the sole male heir of the Tudor dynasty left this world? It gets complicated, so let's have a look at the family tree, starting with Henry VII's surviving children, from oldest to youngest:

1. **Arthur**—He'd been married to Catherine of Aragon for a short time and died before they could have any children. She moved on to the next son in line.
2. **Henry VIII**—He changed England's history forever by breaking with Rome, all to try to have a son, who was now on his deathbed. Could those daughters finally come in handy? Elizabeth, who had an unvoiced religious bent, had been declared illegitimate when his marriage to Anne Boleyn was conveniently wiped off the books so that he could marry Wife #3, Jane Seymour (doomed Edward's

Dynastic Dysfunction

A visual guide to how the heck this all happened

Edward the Black Prince
d. 1376
m.
Joan of Kent
d. 1385

John of Gaunt
Duke of Lancaster
d. 1399
m.
1. Blanche
of Lancaster
d. 1369

3. Catheri
Swynfor
d. 1403

RICHARD II
d. 1400
m.
1. Anne
of Bohemia
d. 1394
2 Isabella
of France
d. 1409

HENRY IV m. 1. Mary de Bohun
d. 1413   d. 1394

2. Joan of Navarre
d. 1437

2. Constance
of Castile
d. 1394

HENRY V m. Catherine of Valois
d. 1422   d. 1437
m.
Owen Tudor
d. 1461

John Beaufort m. Margaret Holland
Earl of Somerset   d. 1439
d. 1410

John Beaufort m. Margaret of Bletsoe
Duke of Somerset   d. 1482
d. 1444

HENRY VI
d. 1471
m. Margaret of Anjou
d. 1482

Edmund Tudor m. Lady Margaret Beaufort
Earl of Richmond   Countess of Richmond
d. 1456   d. 1509

Boom! there it is!

HENRY VII
d. 1509

Arthur
Prince of Wales
d. 1502
m.
Catherine of Aragon

HENRY VIII
d. 1547
m.

Margaret Tudor
d. 1541
m.

1. Catherine of Aragon
d. 1536
Divorced 1533

2. Anne Boleyn
d. 1536
Executed

3. Jane Seymour
d. 1537
Executed

1. James IV
of Scotland
d. 1513

2. Archibald
Earl of Angus
divorced
d. 1557

3. Henry Stewart
Lord Methven
d. 1552

MARY I
d. 1558
m.
Philip II of Spain

ELIZABETH I
d. 1603

EDWARD VI
d. 1553

James V
of Scotland
d. 1542
m.

Lady Margaret Douglas m.
Countess of Lennox
d. 1578

Matthew Stuart
Earl of Lennox
d. 1571

1. Madeleine
de Valois
d. 1537

2. Mary of Guise
d. 1560

Mary Queen of Scots
d. 1587

The Red Rose is associated
with the Lancasters

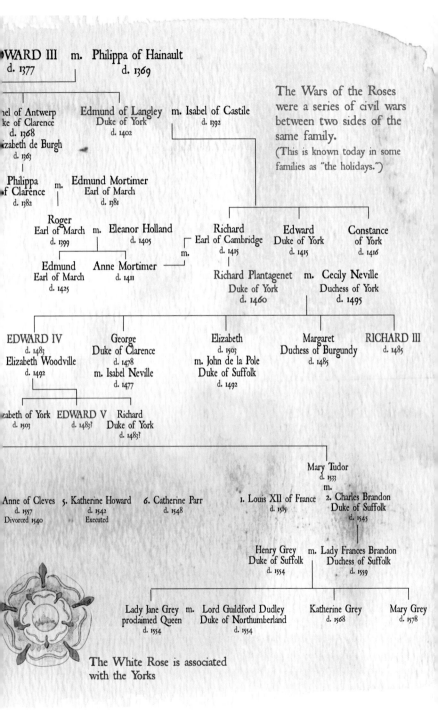

WARD III m. Philippa of Hainault
d. 1377 d. 1369

Edmund of Langley m. Isabel of Castile
Duke of York d. 1392
d. 1402

The Wars of the Roses were a series of civil wars between two sides of the same family.
(This is known today in some families as "the holidays.")

hel of Antwerp
ke of Clarence
d. 1368
izabeth de Burgh
d. 1363

Philippa m. Edmund Mortimer
f Clarence Earl of March
d. 1382 d. 1381

Roger
Earl of March m. Eleanor Holland
d. 1399 d. 1405

Richard
Earl of Cambridge
d. 1415
m.

Edward
Duke of York
d. 1415

Constance
of York
d. 1416

Edmund
Earl of March
d. 1425

Anne Mortimer
d. 1411

Richard Plantagenet m. Cecily Neville
Duke of York Duchess of York
d. 1460 d. 1495

EDWARD IV
d. 1483
Elizabeth Woodville
d. 1492

George
Duke of Clarence
d. 1478
m. Isabel Neville
d. 1477

Elizabeth
d. 1503
m. John de la Pole
Duke of Suffolk
d. 1492

Margaret
Duchess of Burgundy
d. 1485

RICHARD III
d. 1485

izabeth of York
d. 1503

EDWARD V
d. 1483?

Richard
Duke of York
d. 1483?

Mary Tudor
d. 1533
m.

Anne of Cleves
d. 1557
Divorced 1540

5. Katherine Howard
d. 1542
Executed

6. Catherine Parr
d. 1548

1. Louis XII of France
d. 1515

2. Charles Brandon
Duke of Suffolk
d. 1545

Henry Grey m. Lady Frances Brandon
Duke of Suffolk Duchess of Suffolk
d. 1554 d. 1559

Lady Jane Grey m. Lord Guildford Dudley
proclaimed Queen Duke of Northumberland
d. 1554 d. 1554

Katherine Grey
d. 1568

Mary Grey
d. 1578

The White Rose is associated with the Yorks

mom). Who was left? Mary, his daughter with Catherine of Aragon, was a Catholic. Less than ideal.

3. **Margaret**—She'd been sent up to Scotland to marry James IV. Their granddaughter was Mary Queen of Scots, another Catholic and not a direct threat at that point since Henry's Catholic daughter Mary was closer in the line of succession. But don't forget about this Scottish Mary! She'll be important when (a) Elizabeth becomes queen and has to ensure that there are no threats to her crown, and (b) after Elizabeth dies childless. That's some time away, though.

4. **Mary**—She married Charles Brandon and had a daughter, Frances, who married a Mr. Henry Grey. Together they had a little girl named Jane.

This is where Lady Jane Grey came in. As far as Edward VI was concerned, this strong-minded and clever girl was the only legitimate Protestant anywhere near the line of succession, the great-granddaughter of Henry VII.

The problem was, Henry VIII's last word on next-in-line, the Third Succession Act of 1543, had been approved by Parliament. It named Mary and Elizabeth after Edward. Yet Edward, steered by his protector, crafted his own ending to the story. He called it his Devise for the Succession and named tiny teen-aged Jane Grey as his heir. Only then would the country have any chance of remaining Protestant. Young Edward was a religious fanatic so he was all over this, not that he had much energy left to argue. However, his plan didn't get the thumbs-up from Parliament, and that made all the difference down the line.

When the pale fifteen-year-old girl learned that she was queen, it was reported that she felt "stupefied and troubled" and fainted straightaway. She came back to her senses momentarily and realized that the others in the room—her parents as well as her father-in-law, John Dudley, Duke of Northumberland—had stood around like bumps on a log and didn't even help her, and then she began to cry right there on the floor.

After she'd finally gotten herself together, it's believed she said, "The crown is not my right and pleaseth me not. The Lady Mary is the rightful heir." Well, that settles that, right? Not even close, but she eventually took on her new role as professionally as could be expected.

For nine days, anyway. During that time, Mary (who had fled to Framlingham Castle after Edward VI's death) showed up in London with a vengeance and planned to take the crown back for herself. Jane was imprisoned, and the stress made her ginger hair fall out and gave her flaky skin. But that was going to be small potatoes next to losing her head the following February. Seven months from her imprisonment, she found herself kneeling before the chopping block. Turned out she'd had her work cut out for her, after all.

It wasn't bad enough to have been beheaded, but poor Jane had a stressful last few moments of her life as well. She was blindfolded and then worriedly asked the executioner, "Will you take it off before I lay me down?" His answer was no, so she attempted to lay her head on the block.

Not that she could *see* where the block was, being blindfolded and all. The crowd froze as she waved her arms around in the air, feeling for the surface and in a panic asking, "What shall I do? Where is it??" A kind bystander guided her hands to the block and that was the last Jane knew of this life.

6

Mary I:
Bringing Catholic Back

For a queen, it's not all jewels and castles and ordering the death of your enemies. Mary I was a tragic historical figure who just couldn't seem to catch a break. Although she wasn't the longed-for son, little Mary was a happy, affectionate, and intelligent girl. Older Mary, however, was embittered by events that would have stung anyone, let alone a teenager already prone to misery because of frequent headaches and crippling menstrual pain.

Her father divorced her dear mother, Catherine of Aragon, and she had to watch as Anne Boleyn sashayed into her father's life. Mary and her mother were practically demoted to riff-raff, and forbidden even to see each other for five years—to the day of her mother's death.

Soon after, she had to wait on her little half-sister Elizabeth like a common servant. Her father disinherited her and she was no longer in line for the throne. But this changed after Anne Boleyn lost her head: Elizabeth was the one removed from the succession. Henry's next gal, Jane Seymour, showed affection for his older daughter and convinced Henry to reconcile with her. But he only agreed to this after she signed the "Yep, I'm a bastard!" decree as forced by Dad. She hadn't bothered to read it first; she was simply trying to survive. If anyone could have used a therapist, it was Mary.

As a young lady, the princess was a fashion hound, though she insisted on choosing her own wardrobe. She was an enthusiastic dancer and enjoyed gambling with the ladies of the court—hardly the fuddy-duddy sourpuss of popular persuasion. Like her siblings, she was an academic star. But by the time she'd pulled the rug out from beneath Lady Jane Grey and claimed the crown for herself, she was thirty-seven years old, unmarried, and on her way to being crabby. Around the time of her coronation, she was described as "a very good creation, though rather older than we'd been told," "a perfect saint," "dresses badly," "no eyebrows," "old and flabby . . . It will take a great God to drink this cup." Ouch.

When she'd finally spent some time as queen after all, she lost Calais, England's last bit of land in France. She tortured herself with regret and declared in her surprisingly deep voice, "When I am dead, and my body is opened, ye shall find 'Calais' written on my heart." On the plus side, the crown actually *strengthened* under Mary. Her council began to mend the financial mess her father caused, and started improving the roads, which was good news for trade.

After she took the throne, the bells, incense, crosses, and candles made a reappearance in houses of worship. And yet, proud Mary was Catholic in a land that was slowly turning to Protestantism. Like her successors, Elizabeth and all the kings of the Stuart dynasty, which followed the Tudors, she had built-in enemies who disagreed with her religious beliefs and were constantly plotting to kill her over it. Her own supporters continually encouraged her to execute her half-sister Elizabeth, but she couldn't bring herself to do the deed.

What she could bring herself to do was burn Protestants, and lots of them. Mary sent these souls up in flames because their perceived heresy was treason against God and Her Majesty. She believed she was performing some sort of charity in saving her wayward subjects from themselves. It's easy to see shades of her grandmother, Isabella of Castille, who whipped out the Spanish Inquisition on Moors and Jews, rationalizing that her actions were for the sake of Spain and the souls of the righteous.

Bound by duty to God and country to lead her people back to the Catholic Church, Mary left a stain on her reign and is referred to as Bloody Mary as a result. She was alone in her zeal to send those wayward subjects to the stake. Bishop Gardiner was copacetic with the first few as he believed they'd serve as an example, but they only seemed to increase the faith of the persecuted. The crowds went wild for the willing martyrs, who only brought more enthusiasm for the new religion, not less.

In an effort to bring Catholicism back with a bang, she married a widower who probably never loved her, Philip II of Spain. A political match, their marriage underscored one of the chief problems with a woman

inheriting the throne: England's vulnerability in the hands of a foreign male spouse. In their four years of marriage, Philip barely spent any time with her, so it was no shocker that they never produced an heir. Unbeknownst to her, Mary couldn't have children, but that didn't stop her from convincing herself she was pregnant several times. The final time she thought she had a baby growing inside her, the growth turned out to be a cancerous tumor. That was it for Mary, at age forty-two.

7

Elizabeth I:
The Grand Finale

Although Henry VIII had been hoping for a tiny codpiece in his newborn's layette, Anne Boleyn gave birth to a healthy baby girl who became one of Britain's most iconic monarchs. The birth announcement for the future Elizabeth I (her name honored both of her grandmothers) even shows where "prince" was hastily tweaked to "princess," as hopes for a boy had crumbled.

Elizabeth was in the precarious position of being queen during a tumultuous time in England's history, and she could not flub it up. And it was a veritable miracle that she got to that point to begin with, when we consider how this story unfolded:

- Once upon a time, Henry VIII was married to Catherine of Aragon, and they were supposed to live happily ever after. As we know, that didn't work out, though a daughter (the future Mary I) was born.
- Elizabeth came next, to Henry and Anne Boleyn. But she was still a girl, and that wouldn't do.

- Henry finally found his heir in little Edward, his son with Jane Seymour! By this time, Anne Boleyn's reputation had been trashed and her little daughter deemed illegitimate.
- Edward did succeed his father, but eventually he was one sick puppy and died at the age of fifteen.
- Next up: Mary I! Unhappy marriage, no heirs, cancer consumed her, and only then . . .
- "The queen is dead, long live the queen!" After Mary I lost her battle with something assumed to have been uterine cancer, her half-sister Elizabeth grabbed the reins.

According to the tale, the tall and slim twenty-five-year-old Elizabeth had been lounging under an oak tree at her residence of Hatfield House. The royal courtiers arrived from London on their horses to announce that she was now the queen. She responded in Latin, quoting the 118th Psalm, "It is the Lord's doing, and it is marvelous in our eyes." She was humble and yet commanding from the very beginning.

Henry's younger daughter was formally crowned at Westminster Abbey on January 15, 1559. This became The Magic Date on the counsel of her astrologer John Dee, who advised her that her reign would be "glorious and prosperous" should her ceremony take place on that day.

Elizabeth's coronation was an over-the-top affair, as grand as could be, and certainly banged it into the people's heads that she really was the legitimate queen. (Remember that her own father wasn't even meant to be king; he only stepped in when his older

brother Arthur died.) But on that snow-covered January day, the woman who was arguably England's greatest monarch donned an awesome gold and crimson velvet number, trimmed in ermine, and accepted her crown.

If the stars were aligned to favor her long and successful reign, her enviable combination of personality traits lent a hand as well. She was a linguistic marvel, having mastered possibly nine languages, including Welsh, Irish, Cornish, French, and Italian. An unusually pensive child who was intelligent and loved to learn, Elizabeth matured into an organized and methodical woman. *Could she rule as well as a man?* was the question at the time. The answer now may be, *Even better!* Her own view of how a woman could rule was greatly shaped by watching her stepmother, Catherine Parr, in action when Henry VIII spent a summer in France, leaving the details of the reign in the capable hands of his queen back at home. His youngest daughter had been taught, however, to never speak of her infamous mother in public, and she kept to that for the rest of her life.

During her reign, Elizabeth was indeed the center of the universe. Those in her favor enjoyed the glittering lights of notoriety and approval. Those out of her favor found themselves in a cold, dark place. Her legendary temper spurred reports that she had lashed out at others with her fists and boxed their ears, threw a slipper at Francis Walsingham, and slapped the nervy Robert Devereux clear across his face. She was an indecisive procrastinator as well, which was ironic when considering that she's viewed as one of the greatest leaders in history.

An enthusiastic patron of the arts, Elizabeth was a famous supporter of William Shakespeare (it didn't hurt that his plays flattered her greatly), and the miniaturists Nicholas Hilliard, Isaac Oliver, and his son Peter Oliver. A true Tudor, Elizabeth inherited her father's musical gene, clear from her love of singing, dancing, and playing the virginal, one of which she used is on display at the Victoria and Albert Museum in London.

Charming, mercurial, witty, wise, manipulative, powerful, enigmatic—there's no shortage of descriptors for the last of the Tudor monarchs, who ruled for forty-five years. Alone. Theories on her choice to remain single have abounded for centuries:

Theory 1: She saw how marriage worked out for her mother and stepmothers. Anne Boleyn was so crazy about Henry she lost her head. Jane Seymour was simply dying to be Henry's wife. Anne of Cleves was out-and-out unfriended for a bit. Katherine Howard? Separated from her questionable number of brain cells in no time.

Theory 2: Being a wife had to equal being a mom, and that wasn't always ideal. It killed Jane Seymour, and was indeed a common cause of death for women at that time. Plus, a male child would immediately upstage the queen, as males were considered superior. Elizabeth was not about to swallow that, for her ego as well as for her security on the throne.

Theory 3: Marrying a foreign gent was a potential political minefield, in the religious climate of the sixteenth century. Elizabeth kept her religious preferences private, and putting a preference out there by marrying a Protestant or a Catholic would unwisely open up a can of worms.

Theory 4: Marrying *any* gent meant he'd have a leg up on her (again, that male superiority in action). As can be imagined, that wasn't an option for our independent lady.

Theory 5: The right guy never came along. Popular opinion holds that the closest Elizabeth came to The One was Robert Dudley, whose father was executed for supporting the "Let's Make Lady Jane Grey the Queen!" campaign. Robin, as Elizabeth affectionately called him, was already married, though, so that was terribly inconvenient. Even if he weren't, see Theories 1, 2, and 4.

The queen known as Gloriana either learned remarkably well from others' mistakes, had a natural gift for leadership, or a combination of both. She knew when to stand her ground and when to give in gracefully, at least as far as English history gives her credit. Her quote "I do not wish to make windows into men's souls" is famously cited as proof of her remarkable religious tolerance. Irish Catholics may have disagreed, considering that her subjects in "that rude and barbarous nation," to use the queen's description, suffered their fair share of bloodshed under her watch. Jesuits, too, may have disagreed with her declaration of tolerance, as she had their priests executed for treason under a statute she passed in 1585.

But here's the rub: If Elizabeth had been too sympathetic toward Catholics, she'd have endangered her own claim to the throne by confirming the notion that her own parents weren't lawfully married after all.

MARY QUEEN OF SCOTS

Speaking of Catholics, we have Mary Queen of Scots, a thorn in Elizabeth's side through much of her reign. Mary was Elizabeth's cousin, the granddaughter of Henry VIII's sister Margaret, who'd been sent up to Scotland to marry James IV back at the beginning of the sixteenth century. Initially, Elizabeth respected that Mary was a queen in her own right and was sympathetic to her cousin's predicament with the Protestants of Scotland, who were led by the misogynistic reformer John Knox.

For English Catholics, Mary was the rightful queen. She even displayed England's royal arms with those of Scotland. And this was exactly why she was a huge threat.

Regents had ruled in little Mary's place because she was just a wee lassie of six days old when her father, the flamboyant and pretentious James V, died and passed the Scottish crown to her. Originally promised to the young Prince Edward, son of Henry VIII, Mary was instead sent to France as a five-year-old to be brought up by the French royal family and eventually marry the heir apparent, Francis.

She became an attractive, cultured teenager and was married to her teen dauphin for just over a year when Francis died. *Mon dieu!* Raised as a French girl,

this widow was a foreign stranger to her people in Scotland when she returned, and there she married twice more. A political uprising forced her to abdicate in favor of her infant son, James. On the road again! This time, she fled to England, where Elizabeth I promptly kept her imprisoned for nineteen years in a wide variety of castles, which hopefully staved off any boredom.

After so many years, the good news was that her days as a prisoner were coming to an end. The bad news: it was because she had a date with the executioner. Mary had made the mistake of okaying a plot to assassinate Elizabeth, and she did so in writing. Her letter was intercepted and she took off on her last trip—to Fotheringhay Castle for her trial. Her insistence that English common law didn't apply to a monarch such as herself was a case of "too bad, so sad." The hard evidence of her letter trumped any social standing she believed she had.

Elizabeth vacillated greatly on deciding to execute this cousin she'd never even met, but she eventually signed the warrant. Then, after the ax had shortened the six-foot Scottish queen, Elizabeth went ballistic and blamed everyone but herself for the execution.

Throughout her reign, Elizabeth surrounded herself with loyal, highly competent, and charismatic folk, so there was no shortage of people to blame for any given mishap. Some of those in her close circle included the following:

Francis Walsingham had been hiding out in mainland Europe while Mary I reigned, then returned to

England when her half-sister took the throne, giving Protestants a chance to breathe again. He climbed through the ranks and eventually became Elizabeth's secretary of state. A staunch Protestant, he had an enthusiastic drive for thwarting Catholicism and arranged for the interception of Mary Queen of Scots' correspondence, which led to her aforementioned arrest and beheading. Walsingham also held the dramatically named role of spy-master, granting him carte blanche to sniff out priests and other traitors, which he did exceedingly well, even without the cachet of fancy gadgets, a three-digit codename, and an Aston Martin.

Robert Devereux was to become Elizabeth's favorite later in her life. A rather cocky and defiant youth (who, let's be honest, could come off as an obnoxious brat) was a nobleman and the son of Lettice Knollys, who later married Robert Dudley and got herself ejected from court by a certain green-eyed and possessive queen. Devereux was disgraced when he and his 16,000 troops failed to quash the rebels in Ireland, and it certainly didn't help that he then led a coup against Elizabeth. This childish man naturally fell from grace and lost his inflated head in the process.

William Cecil, a discreet and patient fellow, had known Elizabeth since her early teens. The Cambridge-educated lawyer got his feet wet at Tudor court under the boy king, Edward VI, and became Elizabeth's secretary of state on the first day of her reign. He not only was her chief adviser, he also became

a close friend to whom she'd refer as her "spirit." His fervent Protestantism was front and center (in marked contrast to his colleague Nicholas Bacon, who lived by "safety in moderation" when it came to religious matters). Wise and decisive, he was just what was needed in a time of quick changes and careful decisions. Although he was quite ill into his late seventies, the queen wouldn't hear of his resignation. She had no choice but to let him go when he died five years before she did.

THE SPANISH ARMADA

Just like a lot of people, the final Tudor had in-law trouble, specifically with her brother-in-law Philip II of Spain. He'd been grudgingly married to her half-sister, Mary I, and now he was seriously getting on Elizabeth's last nerve. Granted, he was attractive and stylish and had tons of power in Europe. His Spain was the most powerful country in the world at that time. But he also came off as a bit of a jerk and only stayed married to Mary to further increase his power. In her supporters' eyes, he couldn't have cared less about her and didn't even try to work on a happy marriage.

When Mary died and Elizabeth took the throne, Philip thought he could just swoop in and marry the new queen, but she shot him down the way she eventually shot every other suitor down. He hightailed it back to Spain and, for a while, kept the peace with England, but only for political reasons. He kept hoping England would sway back toward Catholicism,

but his hopes were dashed for good when Mary Queen of Scots (who played for Team Catholic also) was executed by Elizabeth's people in 1587. Yep, that'll do it. At that point, his to-do list went something like this:

1. Get rid of Elizabeth.
2. Make it hip once more to be Catholic in England.

Philip sent the Spanish Armada, which simply refers to the Spanish navy, up against the English navy in the spring of 1588. But in just a few short months, the Spanish, with 8,000 sailors on 130 ships, were defeated not only by the English ships but also by disease and horrible weather conditions. There was a little Ice Age going on, and the weather on the ocean was very hard to take, especially if you were accustomed to sunny Spain. Score one for Elizabeth and Protestantism!

THE END

When people finally got to meet the Virgin Queen late in her life, they were shocked to come face-to-face with a ginger-wigged, black-toothed, knobby old lady who'd stuff a perfumed cloth into her mouth before meeting callers. You couldn't blame them for being surprised. Portrait artists never had the chance to portray her accurately as she aged. Five years into her reign, she put the kibosh on unflattering representations of herself. Three decades later, she ordered the obliteration of any poor portraits that had snuck past despite her image-engineering efforts.

About a month before her death, her rheumatism started acting up in a big way. Her last public appearance came at this time, and after that, it was all downhill. Her dear friend, the countess of Nottingham, had died, and Elizabeth was grieving her terribly. Then the poor queen's joints were so swollen from rheumatism that her coronation ring had to be sawn off her finger. To her, this symbolized the end of her reign.

She spiked a fever by March, and ulcers swelling in her throat eventually segued into pneumonia or bronchitis. On top of everything, she was extremely depressed and simply could not sleep. One week before her death, she was emaciated and often silent.

T minus twenty-four hours or so, the childless queen mimed a crown above her head with her fingers, letting her advisers know she wanted to be succeeded by James VI of Scotland. He was Mary Queen of Scots' son and had been the king of his country for thirty-six years already. That kind of on-the-job experience was hard to top.

Elizabeth knew her time was just around the corner so she asked the archbishop to pray at her bedside on that rainy night. Undoubtedly, she was comforted by his confidence that "though she had been long a great queen here on earth," she'd "soon yield an account of her stewardship to the King of kings." The oldest monarch ever to rule the country at that point, she died just before three o'clock the following morning, ending an era of tremendous accomplishment and drama—the Golden Age of England.

REMEMBER
BEFORE *God* ALL
THOSE WHO,
DIVIDED AT THE
Reformation
BY DIFFERENT
CONVICTIONS,
LAID DOWN
THEIR LIVES FOR
Christ AND
CONSCIENCE SAKE.

*the inscription at the half-sisters'
tomb in Westminster Abbey*

BLOODY MARY VERSUS GLORIANA

If someone has a bad reputation, it can mean that:

- They did things to deserve their reputation.
- They angered their enemies, who in turn fabricated stories that were whispered to everyone they knew, and then may have written history books to trash them for generations to come.

The Tudor queens Mary I and Elizabeth I were on opposite sides of the spectrum, and therefore natural enemies. (When they were younger, they were probably closer to being "frenemies.") Mary was Catholic; Elizabeth most likely would not have identified herself as such. When Mary became queen, some people in England were just getting used to the idea of Protestantism. The girls' father, Henry VIII, had broken with Catholic Rome to marry Elizabeth's mother, Anne Boleyn. This created the Church of England, and the country was no longer dependent on Rome— a good thing in some people's eyes. But when Mary became queen, Catholicism was front and center again, which not everyone liked, especially when being Protestant could mean a one-way ticket to the local hot spot (the stake).

When Elizabeth became queen, she answered with a resounding "Amen!" when prayers for the return of Protestantism were offered during her coronation festivities. However, she couldn't get on board with the idea of married priests, and she enjoyed the extravagant musical compositions that usually accompanied a Catholic mass. Her private chapel held a silver crucifix for which she offered neither explanation nor apology.

Yet, ultimately, she nudged Rome out the back door once again and returned England to a cozy place for Protestants to be. Although she initially fined and jailed some Catholics, she had others executed. Many sources attest that she did this only after there were threats on her life. Others say she killed more Catholics than Mary killed Protestants, but Mary is the one with the nickname Bloody Mary and Elizabeth is forever preserved in history books as Gloriana, a flattering title indeed. Why is this? A few things to keep in mind:

1. Catholic versus Protestant was a huge deal during this time period in England. For some, the country, sadly, was losing a religion it had identified with for ages. For others, hooray!—the country was losing a religion it had identified with for ages! If England were Catholic, as it was in Mary's reign, certain other countries, such as France and Spain, were allies (which helped for political reasons). If England were Protestant, these countries became their enemies. So there was no "Kumbaya, everyone's religion is okay."

2. The queen on the throne, whether Mary or Elizabeth, had to think about her enemies and who had the power to kick her off that throne. At the time, executing those who could kick you off the throne was simply good politics and kept the country stable.

3. John Foxe's *Book of Martyrs*, initially published in
   1563, became nearly as popular with Protestants
   as the Bible was. He reckoned that close to 300
   Protestants were burned at the stake during the
   "horrible and bloody time of Queen Mary." Its bias
   toward the new religion is unmistakable, demon-
   izing Catholics for persecuting Protestants despite
   the fact that Catholics were victims of vigorous
   persecution under other Tudor monarchs.

For example, the 1536 uprising known as the Pilgrimage of Grace rocked Henry VIII's legacy when tens
of thousands of northerners who were devoted to the
old faith, furious about the Dissolution of the Monasteries, decided they weren't going to take it anymore.
Henry had hundreds of the rebels executed, easy
peasy. He had no trouble showing off a ring he'd had
made from a huge ruby that had graced St. Thomas
Becket's obliterated tomb in Canterbury cathedral,
and added insult to injury by burning Becket's bones
in the city center. When Edward VI was England's
king, over 5,000 were killed in the brutal Prayer Book
Rebellion in the southeast in 1549, a reaction to new
laws which essentially scrubbed traditional Catholic
symbols and prayers from worship.

Elizabeth frequently gets a pass for her actions,
due to the idea that she was making decisions for the
good of the country. On the other hand, her father
seemed to be pushing for change to advance his personal agenda. But couldn't one assume that the goal
of producing a male heir was also for the good of the
country (at least in the eyes of a sixteenth-century

king)? Her sister's persecution of Protestants seemed to have been based solely on religion, but there's an argument that she was not only attempting to save their souls but also trying to steer England back to its roots (again, in the country's best interest).

When Elizabeth died and James I (who was James VI of Scotland at the time; see our final chapter) became the new king, Protestantism was very much supported in England and each monarch from James onward needed to remember that to prevent England from flipping its collective lid. James and his next few successors (Charles I, Charles II, and James II) either tolerated Catholicism in England or downright wanted to welcome it back. In 1701, England finally passed an act to guarantee that a Catholic could never again be the monarch.

England has been defined by Protestantism (specifically the Church of England) ever since, and the sweeping majority of history books that had been written about Mary and Elizabeth favored the Protestant-friendly queen over the Catholic one. Regardless of how bloody her own reign may have been, triumphant Elizabeth went down in history as Gloriana, and unpopular Mary became Bloody Mary.

8

Full Circle:
Life After Tudors

With Elizabeth's death in 1603, the Tudor line ended and the Stuart line began with James I. Well, he was James VI of Scotland but was repackaged as James I of England and Ireland. Why?

Scotland had had a separate monarchy since the ninth century, when it became its own country. Elizabeth's successor was the sixth James to be king of Scotland. He was only thirteen months old when his mother, Mary Queen of Scots, was whisked away and later imprisoned and made a head shorter. Little James VI had adults to rule for him, of course, until he reached the age of majority. But he was technically the king of Scotland for thirty-six years before swinging on down to London as the new top dog. Because England had never had a King James previously, he became James I there. He stands out in post-Tudor history as a survivor of the failed Gunpowder Plot devised by Guy Fawkes and friends, as well as the impetus behind the new translation of the Bible, now dubbed the King James Version (or more commonly the KJV, for the succinctly inclined).

And why do we sometimes see Life After Tudors spelled Stewart rather than Stuart? The Scottish dynasty was originally named Stewart, way back in the ninth century. But Mary Queen of Scots grew up in France. There was no *w* in the French alphabet at the time, and she would have spelled it Stuart. Scotland and France were tight during the Tudor period and occasionally beyond that, so Stewart and Stuart were used inter-changeably to describe that post-Tudor dynasty, depending on whether the Scots and the French were playing nicely. (Now it is usually spelled Stuart.) Either way, it spelled d-r-a-m-a f-r-e-e, at least until the Gunpowder Plot of 1605, from which James I narrowly escaped assassination.

And that's drama for a different book!

Who, What, and When: A Tudor Timeline

The Tudor dynasty lasted for 118 exciting years. These are some of the more notable events of the era and when they occurred. (Where dates are incomplete, they are unknown.)

1457
January 28—The future Henry VII is born at Pembroke Castle in Wales to Edmund Tudor and Margaret Beaufort.

1466
February 11—Elizabeth of York is born at the Palace of Westminster to Edward IV and Elizabeth Woodville.

1485
August 7—Henry Tudor defeats Richard III in battle at Bosworth Field and becomes HENRY VII.
December 16—Catherine of Aragon is born at the palace of the archbishop of Toledo, near Madrid, to Ferdinand II of Aragon and Isabella I of Castile.

1486
January 18—Henry VII marries Elizabeth of York.

September 20—Prince Arthur is born in Winchester to Henry VII and Elizabeth of York.

1491
June 28—Prince Henry (later Henry VIII) is born at Greenwich Palace to Henry VII and Elizabeth of York.

1501
November 14—Prince Arthur marries Spanish princess Catherine of Aragon.

1502
April 2—Prince Arthur dies, probably of tuberculosis, at age fifteen.

1503
February 11—Elizabeth of York dies on her thirty-seventh birthday after giving birth to her last daughter, who also dies shortly thereafter.
August 7—Princess Margaret marries James IV and becomes queen of Scotland.
December 26—Pope Julius gives the okay for Prince Henry to marry his brother's widow, Catherine of Aragon. If only he knew how complicated this would get!

1509
April 21—Henry VII dies at Richmond Palace, possibly from tuberculosis, at age fifty-two. The reign of HENRY VIII begins.
June 11—Henry VIII marries Wife #1, Catherine of Aragon, at Greenwich Palace.

June 24—Henry is crowned king, and Catherine is crowned queen.

1510
January 31—Catherine of Aragon delivers a stillborn daughter.

1511
January 1—Catherine of Aragon gives birth to the ill-fated intended heir, Prince Henry, Duke of Cornwall.
February 22—Baby Henry dies at fifty-two days old.

1513
June 30—Henry VIII invades France.
September 9—James IV of Scotland dies, and James V ascends to the throne.
October—Catherine of Aragon delivers a stillborn son.

1514
October 9—Mary Tudor, sister of Henry VIII, marries Louis XII of France.
November—Catherine of Aragon delivers a stillborn son.

1515
January 1—Louis XII dies "from exhaustions in the bedchamber." Mary Tudor, you saucy minx!
May 13—New widow Mary Tudor marries her brother's close friend, Charles Brandon, Duke of Suffolk.
September 22—Anne of Cleves is born in Düsseldorf, Germany.

1516

February 8—The future Mary I is born at the Palace of Placentia to Henry VIII and Catherine of Aragon.

1517

October 31—Martin Luther nails his Ninety-Five Theses to the door of the castle church in Wittenberg, Germany. Happy Halloween, Holy Father!

1518

November 10—Catherine of Aragon delivers a still-born daughter.

1519

June 15—Elizabeth "Bessie" Blount, mistress of Henry VIII, gives birth to the king's illegitimate son, Henry Fitz-roy, later to become Duke of Richmond and Somerset.

1521

Henry VIII publishes a defense of the seven sacraments, directed at Martin Luther. The German quickly publishes a rebuttal.

October 11—Henry VIII is styled "Defender of the Faith" by Pope Leo X. Irony alert on the way . . .

1522

March 1—Anne Boleyn, back from France, takes part in a masked ball at the English court and becomes a lady-in-waiting to Catherine of Aragon.

1526

Henry VIII and Anne Boleyn begin their courtship.

1528
June—Anne Boleyn contracts sweating sickness but bounces back.

1529
April 19—The term Protestant is coined at the Diet of Speyer, Germany.
May 31 through July 23—A trial in the divorce of Henry VIII and Catherine of Aragon ends in the king's favor.

1531
Thomas Cromwell becomes a member of the king's council.

1532
June 23—Henry VIII signs a secret alliance with Francis I, king of France, against Charles V, Holy Roman Emperor.
July 11—Henry VIII banishes Catherine of Aragon from court. And that's the last time she ever sees him.
October—Henry VIII and Anne Boleyn travel together to Boulogne, France, and likely begin their physical relationship.

1533
January 25—Henry VIII and Wife #2, Anne Boleyn, secretly marry at Whitehall.
March 30—Thomas Cranmer is made Archbishop of Canterbury.
May 23—Cranmer annuls Henry's marriage to Catherine of Aragon.

May 28—Cranmer declares Henry and Anne's marriage valid. Good thing: she was now six months pregnant.

June 1—Anne Boleyn is crowned queen.

July 11—Pope Clement VII "excommunicates" Henry VIII but not formally, probably with the expectation that the king will return to the Church. Good luck with that.

September 7—The future Elizabeth I is born at Greenwich to Henry VIII and Anne Boleyn.

1534

March 23—The pope declares that Henry's marriage to Catherine of Aragon is valid. But the First Act of Succession states that Henry's marriage to Catherine of Aragon has been annulled. Further, it states that only Anne Boleyn's children are eligible heirs.

1535

June 22—Bishop John Fisher becomes Cardinal John Fisher but is then executed.

July 6—Thomas More is executed.

1536

January 7—Catherine of Aragon dies at age fifty, probably of cancer, at Kimbolton Castle.

January 24—Henry VIII is knocked from his horse while jousting, and is unconscious for several hours.

January 29—Anne Boleyn gives birth to a premature son who dies immediately. And it continues downhill from here.

May 15—Anne and her brother, George Boleyn, are tried and convicted of incest and treason.

May 17—George Boleyn, Henry Norris, Francis Weston, William Brereton, and Mark Smeaton are all executed for alleged adultery with Anne.

May 19—Anne Boleyn, probably in her early or mid-thirties, is executed on Tower Green.

May 30—Henry VIII marries Wife #3, Jane Seymour, at York Palace.

June 8—The Second Act of Succession states that Henry VIII's first two marriages are annulled and that his heirs are to be Jane's sons, then the sons of any future wives, then Jane's daughters.

July 22—Henry Fitzroy, the king's illegitimate son, dies at age seventeen at St. James's Palace, possibly of tuberculosis.

1537

October 12—The future Edward VI is born at Hampton Court Palace to Henry VIII and Jane Seymour.

October 24—Jane Seymour, in her late twenties, dies of complications from childbirth.

1538

December 17—Pope Paul III formally excommunicates Henry VIII.

1540

January 6—Henry VIII marries Wife #4, Anne of Cleves, at Greenwich.

July 9—Henry's marriage to Anne of Cleves is annulled. Well, that was quick.

July 28—Thomas Cromwell, fifty-five or so years old, is executed on Tower Green, and Henry VIII marries Wife #5, Katherine Howard, at Oatlands.

1541

November 4—Katherine Howard is imprisoned at Syon.

December 10—Thomas Culpeper and Francis Dereham are executed at Tyburn for having relations with Katherine Howard.

1542

February 10—Katherine Howard is taken to the Tower of London to await her execution.

February 13—Katherine Howard, probably age seventeen or eighteen, is executed at the Tower of London.

December 8—The future Mary Queen of Scots is born at Scotland's Linlithgow Palace to James V and Marie de Guise.

December 14—James V of Scotland dies and is succeeded by his infant daughter, who, at six days old, becomes Mary Queen of Scots.

1543

July 12—Henry VIII marries Wife #6, Catherine Parr, at Hampton Court Palace.

1544

June 8—The Third Act of Succession states that Henry's heir is Prince Edward, then Edward's sons and daughters, then Henry's daughters Mary and Elizabeth, respectively.

1546

February 18—Martin Luther dies of general poor health and advanced age in his hometown of Eisleben.

July 16—Anne Askew and other English Reformers are burned at Smithfield.

1547

January 28—Henry VIII, age fifty-five, dies at the Palace of Whitehall, probably from complications of diabetes. The reign of EDWARD VI begins.

February 20—Nine-year-old Edward VI is crowned.

April—Henry VIII's widow, Catherine Parr, marries his former brother-in-law, Thomas Seymour. At least their holidays shouldn't be much different.

1548

August 30—A daughter, Mary, is born to Catherine Parr and Thomas Seymour.

September 5—Catherine Parr dies at Sudeley Castle of puerperal fever, at about age thirty-six.

1553

May 25—Lady Jane Grey marries Guildford Dudley, son of the duke of Northumberland, at Durham House on the Strand.

July 6—Edward VI, age fifteen, dies at Greenwich Palace, probably of tuberculosis.

July 10—LADY JANE GREY takes the reins for a bit. Don't get too comfortable, Jane.

July 19—Lady Jane Grey is imprisoned in No. 5 Tower Green. Reign of MARY I begins.

November 13—Lady Jane and her husband, Guildford, are tried, found guilty of high treason, and sentenced to death.

1554
February 12—Lady Jane Grey, at about age sixteen or seventeen, is executed on Tower Green.
July 25—Mary I marries Philip II of Spain at Winchester Cathedral.

1557
July 16—Anne of Cleves, age forty-one, dies at Chelsea Manor, probably of cancer.

1558
November 17—Mary I dies at St. James's Palace, probably of uterine cancer, at age forty-two. Reign of ELIZABETH I begins.

1559
January 15—Elizabeth I is crowned.
March 18—Act of Supremacy names Elizabeth I head of the Church of England.

1566
June 9—The future James VI of Scotland, who is also the future James I of England, is born at Edinburgh Castle to Mary Queen of Scots and Henry Stuart, Lord Darnley.

1567
July 24—Mary Queen of Scots is forced to abdicate the throne in favor of her thirteen-month-old son, James.

1568
May 16—Mary Queen of Scots flees Scotland for England, where she is promptly imprisoned on the orders of Elizabeth I.

1577
November 15—Elizabeth I sends Francis Drake on a two-year trip that will make him the first Englishman to circumnavigate the globe.

1585
July—The first English settlement on North American soil is established (briefly, anyway) at Roanoke Island in modern-day North Carolina, under the direction of Sir Walter Raleigh.

1586
October 14—The trial of Mary Queen of Scots for treason begins.

1587
February 8—Mary Queen of Scots, age forty-four, is executed at Fotheringhay Castle.

1588
May—The Spanish Armada sets sail to invade England.
July 29—The English defeat the Spanish Armada.
August 9—Elizabeth gives her rousing speech to the troops at Tilbury: "I know I have the body of a weak and feeble woman, but I have the heart and stomach of a king."

September 4—Robert Dudley dies, possibly of malaria or stomach cancer, at age fifty-six.

1590
April 6—Francis Walsingham dies at about age fifty-eight, possibly of cancer.

1598
August 4—William Cecil, Lord Burghley, dies at age seventy-six, probably of general ill health and advanced age.

1601
February 25—Robert Devereux, second Earl of Essex and former favorite of Elizabeth I, is executed for treason on Tower Green at age thirty-five.
November 30—Elizabeth I addresses Parliament for the last time.

1603
March 24—Elizabeth I, age sixty-nine, dies at Richmond Palace of unspecified causes and advanced age. The Tudor dynasty is supplanted by the Stuart dynasty, originally of Scotland.

Thank You Notes

I have been fortunate to have the support of many family and friends over the course of this project and to them I am thankful. Through social media I have also enjoyed the support of fellow Tudorphiles via Facebook, Twitter, Instagram, Pinterest, and of course my blog tudortutor.com (on which links to the previous four may be found). Thank you all so much for being part of our history-loving community.

I also wish to offer my gratitude to the staff of the Folger Shakespeare Library as well as the staff of the Library of Congress, as they have been most helpful in my research efforts.

I thank Lisa Graves for her brilliant illustrations in this book and for helping to create my "brand" in my social media outlets.

I am grateful for the kind endorsements and support from Dr. Suzannah Lipscomb, Claire Ridgway, and Justin Pollard.

Ironically, history was one of my least favorite subjects in school, until I ended up in Gordon Strycula's U.S. History II class during my senior year in high school. Thank you, Mr. Strycula, for making history relevant and exciting, even at eight thirty in the morning.

My dear friend Jennifer Mariano has encouraged my endeavors and interests ever since we were randomly thrown together as roommates during our freshman year at college, and I thank her for her continued support while I worked on this book.

I thank my son, George, for patiently listening when I start out the day with "Hey, guess who died today in fifteen-something?" and having the gentle tact to tell me when I'm going overboard.

Thank you to my daughter, Caroline, for snapping a splendid author photo, and for indulging me by recalling key information about all of Henry VIII's wives.

My interest in the people and events in this book was piqued by many daytrips to castles and historical houses in England during the time my husband, George, and I lived there, right after we were married. I am grateful to him for his enthusiastic insistence that we get out of our cozy Cambridgeshire home and visit England's plentiful historic locales, as well as for planning our recent return to those sites in London. He understands my need for travel and my quest for learning, and for that—and for his continual encouragement—I cannot thank him enough.

Sources

I'm often asked for Tudor book recommendations that would be great for research or even just a fascinating read for pleasure. Any of the works that follow would fit the bill.

PRIMARY SOURCES:

Documents Illustrative of Church History. Gee, Henry, and William John Hardy, eds. New York: Macmillan, 1896.

Instructions given by King Henry the Seventh to his embassadors, When he intended to marry the young Queen of Naples: together with the answers of the embassadors. London: T. Becket and P. A. DeHondt, 1761.

Letters and Papers, Foreign and Domestic, of the Reign of Henry VIII. Vols 1, 7, 10, 12, and 16. Edited by J. S. Brewer, J. Gairdner, and R. H. Brodie. London: Longmans and Co., 1862–1932.

Select Documents of English Constitutional History. G. B. Adams and H. M. Stephens, eds. New York: The Macmillan Company, 1914.

The Third Volume of Chronicles, beginning at Duke William the Norman . . . to the yeare 1586. London: John Harrison, et al, 1587.

SECONDARY SOURCES:

Ackroyd, Peter. *The Life of Thomas More*. New York: Anchor, 1999.

_____. *London: The Biography*. New York: Anchor, 2000.

_____. *Tudors: The History of England from Henry VIII to Elizabeth*. New York: St. Martin's Griffin, 2014.

Arman, Steve. *Reformation and Rebellion 1485-1750*. Portsmouth, New Hampshire: Heinemann, 2002.

Cannon, John and Ralph Griffiths. *Oxford Illustrated History of the British Monarchy*. Oxford, UK: Oxford University Press, 1988.

Dau, William Herman Theodor. *Luther Examined and Reexamined: A Review of Catholic Criticism and a Plea for Reevaluation*. St. Louis: Concordia, 1917.

De Lisle, Leanda. *Tudor: Passion. Manipulation. Murder. The Story of England's Most Notorious Royal Family*. New York: PublicAffairs, 2013.

Fox, Julia. *Sister Queens: The Noble, Tragic Lives of Katherine of Aragon and Juana, Queen of Castile*. New York: Ballantine Books, 2011.

Fraser, Antonia. *The Lives of the Kings & Queens of England*. London: University of California Press, Ltd., 1999.

_____. *The Wives of Henry VIII*. New York: Alfred A. Knopf, 1992.

Guy, John. *Tudor England*. New York: Oxford University Press, 1990.

Lipscomb, Suzannah. *1536: The Year that Changed Henry VIII*. Oxford, UK: Lion Hudson, 2009.

Penn, Thomas. *Winter King: Henry VII and the Dawn of Tudor England*. New York: Simon & Schuster, 2011.

Plowden, Alison. *The Young Elizabeth*. Gloucestershire, UK: Sutton Publishing Ltd, 1999.

Porter, Linda. *Katherine the Queen: The Remarkable Life of Katherine Parr, the Last Wife of Henry VIII*. New York: St. Martin's Griffin, 2011.

Schwarz, Arthur L. *Vivat Rex! An Exhibition Commemorating the 500th Anniversary of the Accession of Henry VIII*. New York: The Grolier Club, 2009.

Skidmore, Chris. *Edward VI: The Lost King of England*. New York: St. Martin's Griffin, 2009.

Somerset Fry, Plantagenet. *The Kings and Queens of England & Scotland*. London: Dorling Kindersley Limited, 1990.

Starkey, David. *Six Wives: The Queens of Henry VIII*. New York: HarperCollins, 2003.

Telegraph reporters, "*Graphic: Richard III's Injuries and How He Died.*" The *Telegraph*, February 5, 2013, www.telegraph.co.uk/science/science-news/9849541/Graphic-Richard-IIIs-injuries-and-how-he-died.html

Weir, Alison. *The Life of Elizabeth I*. New York: The Ballantine Publishing Group, 1998.

Whitelock, Anna. *Mary Tudor: Princess, Bastard, Queen*. New York: Random House, 2009.

Wooley, Benjamin. *The Queen's Conjurer: The Science and Magic of Dr. John Dee, Advisor to Queen Elizabeth I*. New York: Henry Holt and Company, 2001.

About the Author

Photo by Caroline Alexander

Barb Alexander, as a traveler and resident of England, stood where Anne Boleyn and Katherine Howard were executed, Elizabeth I and Mary I are buried, Edward VI was baptised, Henry VIII feasted, and scores of English monarchs were crowned. She would have asked to try out the Coronation Chair but Westminster Abbey probably frowns upon that sort of thing. Barb holds a master's degree in education and currently lives in Virginia with her husband and their two children.